From Al

A Turkish-American Dialogue

From Anatolia to Appalachia

A Turkish-American Dialogue

Joseph M. Scolnick, Jr.
and N. Brent Kennedy

INTERNATIONAL?

MERCER UNIVERSITY PRESS
MACON, GEORGIA USA

ISBN 0-86554-751-3
ISBN 0-86554-776-9

MUP/H561
MUP/P218

The paper used in this publication meets the minimum requirements
of American National Standard for Information Sciences—
Permanence of Paper for Printed Library Materials, ANSI Z39.48-1984.

Library of Congress Cataloging-in-Publication Data

Scolnick, Joseph M., Jr. (Joseph Mendelsohn), 1940–
From Anatolia to Appalachia : a Turkish-American dialogue /
Joseph M. Scolnick, Jr. and N. Brent Kennedy.
p.   cm.
Includes bibliographical references (p.   ) and index.
ISBN 0-86554-751-3 (hardback : alk. paper) —
ISBN 0-86554-776-9 (pbk. : alk. paper)
1. Turkish Americans—Appalachian Region—History.
2. Appalachian Region—Emigration and immigration—History.
3. Appalachian Region—Ethnic relations.
4. Appalachian Region—Social life and customs.
I. Kennedy, N. Brent, 1950–   . II. Title.
F217.A65F75 2003
975.6'0049435073—dc22
2003020857

Contents

* | * | *

For Harriette Ruth
and Robyn
with appreciation for their support and insight.

* | * | *

Preface

In *From Anatolia to Appalachia: A Turkish-American Dialogue* we present an *emerging* geosocial/political/cultural/economic relationship as opposed to describing or analyzing an already fully developed one. In doing so, we rely heavily on the words of people who have had an active role in this evolving state of affairs. Where this growing relationship will eventually lead is unknown, but its relevance in many ways is of such importance that to fail to understand or leave a record of its establishment and development in its early state would be academically and culturally unsupportable.

In this book, we have set about achieving these objectives. Both of us have been directly involved in the Turkish-Melungeon relationship and our insights and observations from this ongoing experience form important components of the book. We hope this volume will inspire others, on both sides of the Atlantic, to explore further the nuances and implications that arise when two "divided" peoples come together as they seek self-identity and self-dignity.

Joseph M. Scolnick, Jr. and *N. Brent Kennedy*

1

Introduction

Joseph M. Scolnick, Jr.

For readers who know little or nothing about the subject matter, we begin with a concise presentation of the story of the Melungeons as a part of American society and with an outline of what is presently known of their connections with the Ottoman Empire and with modern Turks. After briefly discussing these subjects we will go on to tell, among other things, how this volume came into being, explain its purposes, and describe how it is organized.

Since the story of the Melungeons and their possible, or even likely, Ottoman-Turkish connections is discussed at length by Brent Kennedy in the next chapter, only the bare bones of the subject will be laid out here. It is an arresting story, still in the development stage, with many unanswered questions remaining.

Melungeons are a "mystery people" in American society. They are found in their largest numbers in the Southeastern Atlantic region of the United States. According to the standard histories of the country, they should not exist, but they do. What Americans have been told for decades is that this region in colonial days was populated exclusively by peoples of the British Isles, local Native American tribes, and Blacks. That was it. But there definitely were other peoples in the region.

The Melungeons are apparently mixtures of Caucasian, Native Americans, and Blacks, who as well have genetic links to the entire Mediterranean area, plus, in some instances, Anatolia (the heartland of Turkey), the Caucasus, Central Asia, and Northern India. There is DNA evidence to support this claim as well as other types of evidence that will be discussed later. For generations wherever they lived, these people of complex ancestry were greatly discriminated against in myriad ways, both formally and informally. Many intermarried with settlers of British origin and/or moved west as soon as they could. But the discrimination did not end with unfair, sometimes brutal treatment. It also took the form of a systematic, public denial of their belief of who and what they were. The government informed them that they could not possibly be any of what they believed themselves to be as a people. In short, it was a form of cultural genocide. But in the past decade, they have begun to rediscover their roots, rethink their history, and insist that they be heard. How their ancestors originally came to America is part of the story of this book, as is how they have begun to discover and reclaim their sense of identity.

In the process of uncovering their roots, to the considerable surprise of those engaged in researching them, it was found that one strand led to the area of the old Ottoman Empire and the modern Republic of Turkey. Nobody expected this. It had long been thought that there were links to the western part of the Mediterranean, especially the area we know today as Spain, Portugal, and France . . . but Turkey? This was an exciting development and so that strand of the linkage to the Old World has been vigorously pursued. One of the things discovered is that that link was stronger than anyone at first had thought, although the evidence for it remains inconclusive. The other notable thing was the reception of the Turkish people to the Melungeons. The former tended to be fascinated by the possible link, loved the idea of it, and were eager to develop and expand the connection. And some Melungeons fully reciprocated this desire. So the link is in the process of becoming a relationship that, although still in its early stage, continues to develop. There are many possibilities for the future relationship but it will be what the people involved make of it. It surely will be more fully developed in time.

Why would the Turkish people respond so positively and vigorously to the Melungeon story while the French, Spanish, and Portuguese have found the story of relatively minor interest? The answer is simple but very important. The people of France, Spain, and Portugal already know that they have "relatives" in many parts of the world. The Melungeons merely add a curious drop or two to the mix. But the Turks are not in that position. They love having "kin" in America who were—in however small a way—part of this country's founding. What is more, the Turks and Melungeons are both "divided" peoples. Turkey is of "mixed" ancestry also: partly of Europe, the Middle East, the Caucasus, and perhaps also Central Asia. It all depends on the definition used. The Turks are part of a number of regions but not wholly of any. They know very well what that feels like. And the Melungeons, Americans all, have a very mixed ancestry and a distinct sense of being, to some extent, outsiders in their own societies. Thus, there is a sharing of common feelings and perceptions that do not need to be spelled out. In other words, there is a positive chemistry among these peoples, Turks and Melungeons, that permits them readily to identify with each other. Not surprisingly, this link has received a good deal of attention from some Melungeons.

Discussing the Turkish-Melungeon link and how and why it has developed to date is the single most important purpose of this volume. The relationship is still in its early stages but it is promising. The authors agreed that it could be valuable to have a record of what has occurred thus far and an outline of the direction(s) that relationship might be moving. For some people, this relationship is totally insignificant and unworthy of further consideration. They see history as a matter of kings, presidents, wars, treaties, and so on. But history and life are far more than this. Often out of sight of a nation's leaders and its major communications media are currents in a society that provide most of the threads of the fabric of its life. To focus only on a handful of people and events is to fail almost completely to comprehend a society's texture and its development over time. The Turkish-Melungeon relationship exists and will be of interest to many people, if for no other reason than that it records human interactions across centuries and continents. How better to present this exceedingly tangled story now than through a narrative that emphasizes the words of the people who are actively taking part in it? Their words will tell most of the story presented here.

In conceptualizing this book, we decided it was essential that it be written so as to be readily understandable to a broad audience. There is much about its subject matter that will be of interest to scholars in many fields—too many fields, in fact. But to present this material in a manner that would receive broad scholarly approval threatened to make it at the same time unsuitable for a considerable portion of the audience it was felt would naturally have an interest in and respond to it. Therefore, the book has been constructed in an unusual way.

How is the book organized? Following this introduction, the second chapter presents Brent Kennedy's views about the Melungeons and their Ottoman-Turkish linkage. As the reader will immediately note, this is for Kennedy a personal and deeply felt story. No other person has been involved in the subject in so many ways for so long, and the breadth and depth of his knowledge of many aspects of the subject is unequaled. But Kennedy will also make clear a number of questions that require further study. A good deal is known, but much remains to be uncovered. Both what is known and what yet remains to be determined will be considered in chapter 2. The chapter concludes with a listing of sources for further reading for those readers who wish to delve more deeply into the subject.

Chapter 3 presents additional information in the form of interviews of persons who have taken part in the Melungeon story and/or in its Ottoman-Turkish connection. In no sense are these persons a random sample. They do not represent the Tom, Jane, Osman, or Tansu of the street in America or in Turkey. Each has knowledge and/or a viewpoint that is believed to be important enough to be directly recorded in an interview. Naturally, they express some differences of opinion. This also is part of the story. About half the interviews are with Americans and the rest with Turks and Turkish-Americans. Each person communicates directly in his or her own way.

Brent Kennedy and Joseph Scolnick agreed on who would be asked to contribute to this section and what each person would be asked. Several of these were interviewed directly in Turkey or in the United States. (Brent Kennedy has a doctorate in communications and has conducted thousands of such interviews.) Others communicated their responses to questions in writing. None of the results of the interviews have been edited in any way that threatens to change the meaning of what was said or written. Only one of the interviews was translated from Turkish to English. Each person answering the questions responded freely, as he or she wished. "Answers" range from passing over a question entirely to a quite lengthy response. Care has been taken to maintain the integrity and authenticity of the views presented in this chapter.

Chapter 4 presents further information about the subject of the book in the form of public talks delivered by Brent Kennedy during the past few years, and some newspaper articles that report the DNA findings of Kevin Jones, a professor of biology at the University of Virginia's College at Wise. It is expected there will be some repetition here of material in previous chapters but apart from the articles presenting Kevin Jones's findings, in order to prevent any repetition, only minimal deletions have been made that do not falsify what was stated or written. Nevertheless, some repetition is inevitable, given both the nature of the subject matter and the multiplicity of authors.

Originally it was planned that the talks and newspaper articles of the fourth chapter would be placed in an addendum. There was good reason to consider doing this but it was rejected. Some of the material in chapter 4 should come before, not after the last chapter of the volume. At worst, all this does is to break up the presentation of the material but it will have been noticed long before the reader reaches this chapter that there is hardly anything neat and cleanly structured about this book. It was decided that the immediacy, honesty, completeness, and feeling about the subject might clash with a carefully structured and rigidly applied approach, so the apparently loose structure of the book better permits the subject to be explored with the emphases desired. After all, this book is about people who have not lived neat, tidy lives. We trust the subject matter, as it has been presented here, will come through effectively.

Finally, "The Last Chapter of the Book" is exactly that, no more, no less. It is not a "conclusion": a genuine conclusion for the subject is impossible at this time. Neither is it "final" or "the end." Too much is going on, the subject is alive and ongoing, so calling the concluding section "the last chapter of the book" is no more than a minimal statement of fact.

Furthermore, this writer is not a totally impartial observer of the story presented. Since discussing the Melungeon narrative with Brent Kennedy several times in 1997, this writer visited Turkey three times. As a political scientist whose main field is international relations, he began to read extensively about the Ottoman Empire, the Republic of Turkey, and Turkish affairs of the past decade, especially of its foreign policy. Among other things, he has offered several courses at his college dealing with Turkey and has collaborated with Brent Kennedy about almost every aspect of this book. So he has some points he wishes to make on his own.

One of these points is that the basic narrative can be viewed in many differing ways. It is far more complex than the situation in the fable of the blind men and the elephant. In that story, each blind man touched a different part of the animal, thus each described a different beast. With regard to the matter of the Melungeons, their Ottoman-Turkish linkage, and their presently developing relationship, there are more views than touching that mythical elephant ever brought forth. Some critics will go so far as to deny that there are any people we may call "Melungeons." Some will accept the Melungeons as a group but flatly deny any

Ottoman-Turkish linkage. Still others will accept these points to some degree but reject any value in learning how the Melungeons and Turks are developing a relationship.

Read the book! Read it carefully and think about it. See if it does not appear that what is discussed is more than a figment of someone's imagination. Given the existing state of research about every topic mentioned in these pages, some portions of it will be based less on established fact than others. No matter. Further study will correct these mistakes. Such "course corrections" occur all the time in scholarly endeavors. It is believed that despite some inevitable errors of fact or interpretation, the story is essentially grounded in historical fact, and that, equally important, it will matter to many people who read about it. We are looking at people who have lived, surmounted major and minor difficulties, begun to find themselves, and who are reaching out to others to whom they are related, whether genetically, emotionally, culturally, or psychologically. It is part of the continuing story of mankind. *That* is fully worthy of attention.

Finally, as mentioned above, this is a story of two "divided peoples." Such peoples have existed throughout history but have usually received little attention. But the situation of a person or small group not belonging entirely to one large group or another is increasingly common. This is certainly true in the United States. Large numbers of Americans today are the result of mixed marriages in ethnic, racial, and religious terms. They have multiple heritages. What they lack in the security of belonging entirely to one group they make up for in possessing a broader cultural background and usually an enhanced ability to understand many viewpoints. The Melungeons are such a group, as indeed are most modern Turks, with a complex mix of ethnic backgrounds of their own and a country that uncomfortably straddles cultures and continents.

This book then is about people who are creating *whole* identities for themselves out of multiple backgrounds. Thus, far from being a tale of unusual people in unfamiliar circumstances, this is a story of many of us—the human race. All "divided" people have some stake in the outcome of the story. That also is worthy of attention.

2

Background

N. Brent Kennedy

An Unlikely Source for Turkish-American Diplomacy

Something truly astonishing in the history of Turkish-American relations is unfolding, at first unnoticed by most but now gathering a momentum that seems to guarantee at least some sort of permanent mark on the shared history of these two nations. A burgeoning flotilla of relationships—not at the governmental level, but at the man-and-woman-in-the-street level—is now afloat and appears irreversible in its permutations and increasing complexities. Perhaps what is most astonishing is that this social and cultural phenomenon began not in the nation's capitol, nor in the corridors of the United Nations, nor even in meeting rooms in any of the hundreds of American cities. It was not birthed by some university think tank, nor was it an outgrowth of prior political or economic liaisons between the two countries. Instead, it grew out of a human search for roots and identity that began, and continues to be centered, in the heart of the Appalachian Mountains, one of our nation's poorest and most economically depressed regions. The mixed-ethnic Appalachian people historically known as "Melungeons" are forging the way in this brave new experiment in international relations.

Since 1995, hundreds of Appalachian children in Virginia, Tennessee, and Kentucky have acquired Turkish pen pals, which includes Turks of all ethnic persuasions, from Anatolians to central Asians to Armenians to Kurds. A myriad of cultural exchanges are underway and it is no longer an unusual sight to see native Turkish musicians jamming and dancing with traditional Appalachian fiddlers and singers. The extremely traditional Country Cabin, located outside Norton, Virginia, is a regular site for such unexpected international artistic collaboration. The small Appalachian town of Wise, Virginia, and the Aegean town of Çeşme,

Turkey, improbably won a major Sister Cities International Award for their extraordinary achievements in promoting international understanding on extraordinarily limited budgets. Melungeon and other Appalachian children poured out their hearts and dollars and brand new toys to assist in earthquake relief, following the massive earthquake centering near Izmit, Turkey, on August 17, 1999. WISE-FM and WETS-FM, National Public Radio affiliates at the University of Virginia's College at Wise (UVaWise) and East Tennessee State University (ETSU), jointly sponsored in-depth humanitarian and educational programming during the earthquake crisis. UVaWise has also established sister institution relationships with both Istanbul University and Dumlupinar University. Student exchange programs are now under way. Busloads of Turkish and Turkish-American tourists visit Wise County on a regular basis to participate in the increasingly popular "Melungeon Unions"—combined cultural, genealogical, and academic conferences dedicated to the exploration of Melungeon history and culture. Melungeons visit Turkey annually for Melungeon Heritage Tours. Çeşme has renamed its main street "Wise Caddesi" and the mountain overlooking Çeşme and the Aegean is now called "Melungeon Mountain." Wise has erected an ornate, handcarved sign proclaiming its friendship with the people of Çeşme, and a "fountain of friendship" constructed from handmade ceramic tiles by craftsmen from Kutahya has been promised for the UVaWise grounds. The Melungeon Heritage Association has been accepted as a full member of the Assembly of Turkish American Associations (ATAA), as well as the Portuguese-American Society. UVaWise Jeffersonian scholar Garrett Sheldon has completed a comparative work on the political philosophies of Thomas Jefferson and Mustafa Kemal Atatürk (1881–1938), Ottoman general, Turkish statesman, and first president. UVaWise psychologist Mary Darcy O'Quinn is wrapping up a study comparing self-concepts and levels of confidence between Anatolian and Appalachian women. UVaWise library director Robin Benke is building a Turkish resources collection, and yet another colleague, molecular biologist Kevin Jones, has undertaken a groundbreaking comparative DNA study of Melungeons and their theorized ancestral populations.

Both the American media and the Turkish and Azerbaijani media have leaped on the activities and stories and photo-ops that have resulted from the Melungeon-Turkish courtship. The *Wall Street Journal*, the *Washington Post*, and the *Atlanta Journal-Constitution* all have carried front-page stories on the Melungeons, as have leading Turkish media such as *Sabah, Hurriyet, Zaman,* and *Milliyet.* Radio, television, and Internet coverage have been intense, both here and abroad. Melungeon delegations have visited and interacted with villagers in the most remote sections of central and southern Anatolia, but have also sat with a number of high-ranking governmental officials, such as Süleyman Demirel, Mesüt Yılmaz, and American Ambassador Mark Parris. Beyond governmental personages, the contacts and visits have included figures from both the left and the right, and both secular and Islamic leaders. In ten treks to Turkey, I have enjoyed conversations with the likes of the above, but also—and more importantly—common folk such as the old Turkish fisherman near Kuşadasi who proclaimed his love of Atatürk despite his acknowledgement of Greek origins through his mother's people. In fact, it's the so-called common people on both sides that have made this phenomenon exactly that—a phenomenon. I sat and chatted heart-to-heart with two young Kurdish street vendors outside a mosque in Istanbul, and did likewise with a charming Armenian family in Izmir. I traded family stories with a Jewish rug merchant near Ayvalık and was entranced by the deeply felt origin stories of dark-skinned, blue-eyed Romany (Gypsies) I encountered near Antalya. To me, they were all "Turks" and probably indicative of the human smorgasbord that comprises both modern and Ottoman Turks.

My kinsmen in the Appalachians are enjoying the same life-altering experiences. People to people, heart to heart, soul to soul. At least some of us Melungeons believe ourselves to be partly "Ottoman," but also partly Native American, African, Jewish, and European; that is, we are "Americans" in the modern inclusive sense, just as the above-mentioned "Turks" are likewise an inclusive ethnic brew. We take note of our similarities, and, if only for a moment, brush aside our differences and thus create vast new territory for bonding. When we visited Turkey, no one was "pure" anything—just human beings looking for connections with other human beings. Indeed, this is what the so-called "Melungeon Movement" is truly all about—a grassroots (some would say a "subsoil") social activism committed to rejecting the old way of doing racial business. Melungeons are making an emotional grasp for their past, recognizing their untold history of diversity, and—in an unusual gesture for these times—rejecting anger and compensation for past injustices in return for the unbridled privilege of teaching others what it means to be an American—and to forgive. These people, who believe themselves to be an amalgam of all races (and most certainly can document a menu of social and legal injustices) are among the most patriotic of Americans. There is a recognition that this nation, as imperfect as it has been, and still can be at times, still permits—even encourages—the very introspection that has led to this new-gained sense of pride and self. Our hope is that it will be contagious.

Moving Beyond Oppression and Injustice

What continues to amaze, is that this astonishing cultural phenomenon was birthed by a people considered to be among Appalachia's most impoverished and ill-educated offspring—the Melungeons. Few American ethnic groups have been as reviled as our people. Consider what Nashville journalist Will Allen Dromgoole reported in *The Arena* in 1891:

> The Melungeons are filthy, their home is filthy. They are rogues, natural born rogues, close, suspicious, inhospitable, untruthful, cowardly and, to use their own word, sneaky. In many things they resemble the Negro. . . . They are an unforgiving people, although . . . they are slow to detect an insult, and expect to be spit upon.

As fellow Melungeon and present-day historian Darlene Wilson explained in a May 30, 2000, *Washington Post* article:

> Appalachia is that place where you ain't never gonna get white enough, but spent an incredible amount of time trying. You can't have a middle class unless you've got an underclass. America needed Appalachia the way Appalachia needed Melungeons.

Melungeons, a mixed-race, or mixed-ethnic, population are found in identifiable scattered population pockets throughout the Appalachian Mountains but particularly in eastern Tennessee, southwestern Virginia, and eastern Kentucky. Their less identifiable relatives are even more broadly scattered, most probably not even suspecting their non-Anglo heritage. Wherever the pockets lie, they invariably share a nucleus of the same surnames (for example, Adams, Adkins, Bell, Bennett, Collins, Gibson/Gipson, Goins, Hall, Kennedy/Cannaday, Moore, Mullins, Nash, Osborne, Sexton, and so forth) and possess a centuries-old, and generally unsuccessful, history of proclaiming at least a partial Mediterranean heritage. Wherever they have been found, they have claimed a Portuguese, or Turkish, or even Jewish background which typically subjected them at best to ridicule and at worst to various forms of prejudice, ranging from legal disenfranchisement to outright violent removal or worse. Their history has been punctuated by unspeakable heartache and trauma, not unlike the experience of their Native American and African-American kinsmen, two groups with whom they admixed over time and place. Whoever they may have been—more on that question in the next few pages—the Melungeons were encountered with great regularity by the early and mid-eighteenth-century Scots-Irish as they poured by the thousands into the Shenandoah Valley of Virginia and points farther south. While most were eventually shoved westward, or upward onto the mountaintops, significant numbers—generally Melungeon women—stayed put by marrying the predominantly male settlers that came looking for better lives thousands of miles from Ulster. In this way, their genes were spread far more extensively than most researchers have ever understood. Estimates today are that some 75,000 people enthusiastically consider themselves to be "Melungeon," another two to three million have some inkling of their Melungeon heritage, and millions more, knowingly or unknowingly, carry some degree of the ancestry.

Even with regular intermarriages, however, the majority of Melungeons were still either too dark or at least not quite white enough to pass muster in a New World where skin color bore more relevance than intelligence, drive, and integrity. Beginning in the late 1700s, Melungeons were declared "free persons of color" (FPC) throughout the upper and mid-South and stripped of their rights to vote, marry, attend school, hold a job, own property, or be represented in courts of law. Most migrated westward, trying to pass as "white" (that is, as northern European) and taking on new lives when possible. Their former claims of being, typically, Portuguese ("Portyghee," as they pronounced the term), Turkish, and Jewish soon gave way to the more expedient quest of simply surviving—and surviving meant being English or Scots-Irish or maybe German or "Black Dutch." The vast majority of the Melungeons did indeed manage to "change" their ethnicity, or at least their classification, and melded into the greater American ethnic stew that was anything but homogenous in its origins. But by the late 1900s, governmental and perhaps unwitting academicians had literally "whitewashed" American history. And state-sponsored racism by such men as Virginia's W. A. Plecker, state medical registrar and eugenics proponent, ensured that those

Melungeons who had managed to remain in the Appalachians would be, as he put it, "kept in their place." Plecker, who in the late 1930s had traveled to Germany to assist the Nazis in designing their eugenics movement, was an enthusiastic enforcer of Virginia's Racial Integrity Act, continuing his reign of terror right into the early 1940s. As late as the 1930s he was sending official writs to extreme southwestern Virginia in an attempt to turn children of Melungeon heritage out of the public school systems. The surnames he used to judge a child's "Melungeoness" (or "mongrelism" as he sometimes put it) read like a telephone directory from Wise County, Virginia. His death by means of a Richmond, Virginia bus driver who failed to see him step onto a busy street was the only thing that stopped Plecker from countless more years of what scholars such as J. David Smith have called "documentary genocide." But thanks to Plecker and others like him the damage was done. Melungeons and other mixed-race folks had long since given up their proclamations of self and had slipped into the American way of surviving at all costs. But the legacy of racism and the inescapable cultural memories and physical traits are not so easily stuffed into a drawer and forgotten. (See end of chapter for suggested reading list.)

Rediscovering the True Self

Throughout much of America, and especially in Appalachia, olive-complexioned children were drilled incessantly on their northern European origins and, as a sidebar, that their parents and grandparents were either lying or grossly misinformed on their ancestry. I was one of those children, repeatedly told by teachers of my family's "pure" English and Scots-Irish origins, only to return home each day to experience firsthand, or on-the-ground as we say, the Middle Eastern faces of my family. It was only in the eighth grade when W. G. Bays, a local teacher and football coach, looked our class in the eyes and proudly proclaimed his own nonwhite background. It was an illuminating moment for me, being the kid who had sat in stunned silence in the old Coal-Town Theatre when he realized that his family looked not like the English but instead like the Arabs and Turks in *Lawrence of Arabia*. But W. G. Bays's *Assertion of Native American Ancestry* was the exception, not the rule, and who were we to argue with the majority? The winners write history and we were being given the chance to amalgamate into the winner's circle. Most of us did so, myself included. But in the backs of our minds we still occasionally wondered about those faces, and the oral traditions, and the improbable Mediterranean diseases that kept popping up among a people classified as "triracial isolates"—a mixture of northern Europeans, sub-Saharan Africans, and Native Americans. A people, according to the rules of academia, that possessed *no* Mediterranean heritage but simply the fantasy of belonging to some "exotic" parentage as some academics still inexplicably refer to the most populous empires of the sixteenth and seventeenth centuries—the Spanish and the Ottomans. My visits to old family graveyards where crescent moons and stars of David could—and still can—be seen on the oldest of the tombstones, and where names like Canara, Louisa, Navarrh, Abram, Helena, Didama, Armeni, Samsun, Eulalia, Vardeman, and Isham, were brushed aside as simply the eccentricities of a confused and ignorant mountain folk.

It had taken a while, but by the early 1900s most Melungeons had become Johns and Jacks, and Susans and Sarahs. And there was little talk, except among the adults in closed family quarters, of what used to be and what might have been.

A Lesson in Hidden Diversity

Whoever they were, the Melungeons, save for a few hardy souls (most notably on Newman's Ridge in Tennessee and Stone Mountain in Virginia), have dispersed widely—and generally westward—over the past 250 years. Most blended in with one of the three available classifications of those periods: White whenever possible (again, northern European), Black (sub-Saharan African), or Indian (Native American). And most adopted the cultures of those populations into which they entered. In this respect, the Melungeon odyssey has been carried to all races and most ethnic groups in America. If Pocahontas, who had but one surviving child, could today have, according to some estimates, as many as 150,000 living descendants, how many living Americans could be descended from the hundreds, even thousands, of so-called Melungeons who were documentably on our lands? A lot, to be less than scientific. But American historians set about a century later forcibly stuffing all into nice, neat racial classifications based on political, as opposed to anthropo-logical, criteria. The truth was—and is—that many so-called "Blacks" were not sub-Saharan Africans, many so-called "Whites" were not northern European, and many so-called "Indians" were neither Native American nor Asian. But our nation's unique manner of human pigeonholing influenced several generations of scholars to religiously follow an old suit and, perhaps most tragically, nearly wipe out a multitude of rich ethnic subcultures that played vital roles in building our nation.

Anyone who attends a Melungeon festival will be amazed at the ethnic and racial richness of humanity that calls itself "Melungeon." White, Black, Asian, Indian—they all come to celebrate their common origins and they all revel in a newfound pride in being not only Melungeon, but in being Americans. Contrary to the warnings of some early critics, the Melungeon Movement has not further subdivided an America already obsessed with ethnic and racial purity, but instead has become a model for a new ethnicity based not on skin color or national origins, but instead on shared experience. Which is what nationhood should be about anyway. In fact, the Melungeon credo—splattered on their posters, brochures, websites, and so on, is "One People, All Colors." But for those scholars who insist upon dividing, dividing once again, classifying, and then studying, the inclusiveness of the Melungeons has always been troubling. What they fail to see is that the scholarly penchant—or obsession—to break everything into smaller and smaller units has wreaked havoc on real human beings living real lives on-the-ground. Games of academic one-upsmanship are fine as long as they are confined to the journals, but they can be deadly when used as the fodder for enacting racial integrity laws or defining (from the outside looking in) the identity, the culture, and the nature of other human beings. Equally important is the growing recognition that indeed the winners—and of course usually the wealthy literate among the winners—write history. Modern DNA studies are lending credence worldwide to the so-called origin myths of many ethnic groups who have long been disparaged by academicians—routinely Eurocentrists—who keep demanding, "Show me the documentation!" which can often be translated as "Show me what the northern European victors have written!" There is no better example of this pompous practice than the experience of the South-African Lemba tribe, where DNA analysis now supports their long-standing and agonizingly unsuccessful claim of Semitic heritage.

As I discovered in the early 1990s, and especially after the publication of my "manifesto" in 1994 (*The Melungeons: The Resurrection of a Proud People. An Untold Story of Ethnic Cleansing in America*), my family was not alone in its suffering and its long-tolerated denial of self. Melungeon descendants—and there were many—came out of the

woodwork in a mass catharsis of self-exposure, introspection, reevalua-
tion, celebration, and a determination, at long last, to tell their own stories
as experienced not by outsiders, but by themselves. They have reached
out, as well as backward in time, to embrace who they are and who they
were. And they have reconnected to most of those bits and pieces. The
Melungeon quest for self is much akin to the search an orphaned child
might undertake in seeking its parentage.

This analogy is so crucial to understanding the Melungeon mass
attitude, as well as the Turkish connection itself, that we should take a
moment and play it out.

Understanding the Pull

Imagine for a moment that you are the product of four other human
beings—your maternal and paternal grandparents. Imagine further that
one grandparent is an Englishman, and his wife is Turkish. Imagine that
another grandparent is Portuguese, and her husband is the product of a
Native-American and African-American union. Then imagine you are
unaware of this heritage but are brought up to believe you are merely an
Englishman who has black curly hair, epicanthic folds on your eyelids,
and olive skin. Each day you look in the mirror and know in your heart
that something else is at play. And on occasion you hear the whispered
suggestion from within your own family of non-Anglo origins. But when
you suggest to others on the outside that such might be the case, you are
ridiculed or corrected at best. Inevitably, the reason for your "different-
ness" falls back on you; that is, somehow it's your fault. Something went
wrong with you and specifically with your family's genetics. You are
something of a mistake, something not quite right. (This has indeed been
a widespread and deeply felt sentiment on the part of many Melungeon
families.) Further, imagine that as time goes on, you and other family
members suffer from Machado-Joseph disease (MJD), thalassemia, Tay-
Sachs disease, Behçet's disease, familial Mediterranean fever (FMF),
and/or sarcoidosis. Imagine that you and your family are severely lactose
intolerant and several of your older uncles have had devastating stomach
and intestinal surgeries simply because their physicians misdiagnosed the
simple—but serious—problem of total lactose intolerance. Imagine that
far more serious conditions and diseases are undiagnosed or misdiagnosed
and that your attempts to lead your doctor in a different direction are
dismissed out of hand because he knows American history and is

therefore confident that you cannot have any of these "exotic" diseases. Imagine that you die needlessly of kidney amyloidosis because of undiagnosed FMF, or that you slowly become crippled—as I once was becoming—when a single daily tablet of colchicine can dissipate the agony embedded in your joints and lungs. This is the very real medical legacy of hidden roots, and our growing understanding of this rich diversity is already changing the practice of medicine in the Appalachians, by itself a worthy goal of roots digging.

The search for self goes far beyond an emotional need for genealogical anchors. And we haven't even touched on the need to destroy, or at least erode, the old and very erroneous stereotype of the homogenized Appalachian: a "pure" sandy-haired, freckle-faced, Scots-Irish, fiddle-playing, ignorant, violent, bigoted hillbilly. I grew up on one of the most isolated mountaintops of Appalachia and I never met the above stereotype, though I learned from outsiders in graduate school that he was commonplace in my home region.

In any event, take all the above imaginings and imbibe in one final flight of fancy: at long last you find your four grandparents and in your ecstasy you run to embrace them. While they all acknowledge you as their seed, some are more reticent that others to take you back into the fold. It's been a long time, after all, and people and families move on. But for whatever reason, one grandparent reacts differently. Gives you an extra long look, seems to recognize something, smiles back, and hugs you. Invites you home for dinner and introduces you to your new cousins who also embrace you. While you want the connections with all your grandparents, you also revel in the embrace that is available to you. It's a beginning and if you develop this one, then the others may well follow. And even if they don't, well . . . at least this is partial success in that you are no longer so alone.

In fact, this is what has happened to the Melungeons. After years of being, in the words of one journalist, "nobody at all," suddenly we are akin to all the other "hyphenated-Americans." We, too, have a homeland and a history that is uniquely our own. A basic human need has mercifully been satisfied. It is no different than those "Irish-Americans" who, after a century and a half of admixing with other ethnic groups on these shores, return home again and again to kiss the Blarney Stone. No one ever questions their "Irishness" nor demands a DNA test to admit them to a St. Patrick's Day celebration. But the Irish, though also a historically oppressed people, are at least European and that guarantees them a seat, however modest, at the American family dinner table. The Melungeons have, in essence, decided that they are no longer willing to take their seat under false pretenses. To them, there is nothing inherently wrong in being Portuguese, or Jewish, or African, or Turkish, or any combination thereof. They feel themselves to be as American as every Anglo-American, German-American, Scottish-American, or Irish-American who ever sang the "Star Spangled Banner." They, too, know the words.

Hope for Both Sides

For better or worse, the modern Turks are the legacy bearers of the old Ottoman Empire. This is not to say that modern Turks are the same people as the "Turks" who came to these shores early on, but certainly they form the bridge of continuity that permits the homecoming. This basic human experience—at the level of the people (indeed, the Turkish government has, at least over the first ten years, taken virtually no interest in the subject)—has sufficiently replicated itself on both sides of the Atlantic to the point that there is indeed a social movement afoot. While I receive communications from scholars both here and abroad, their numbers are dwarfed in comparison to the postcards, letters, and e-mails from Americans of all ages either discovering, or further pursuing, their Melungeon heritage. What is equally astonishing is that not a week goes by that I don't also receive dozens more from Turkish citizens of all ages, similarly caught up in the search for connections. All of them, both Americans and Turks, are engrossed in the poignant story of a people's search for self and roots. And perhaps most amazing—and encouraging— is that the letters from the Turks tell us something about the Turkish mindset, a mindset often different from the more publicized "Turkish face" presented by both the Turkish media and official Turkish governmental agencies. These Turks *want* connectivity, not simply to the Melungeons but to one another. They see the Melungeons as a model of sorts—seeming proof that, at least in America and at least centuries ago, Turks and Greeks and Armenians and Kurds and Arabs and Jews and God only knows who else, could somehow unite into a single people and survive oppression and bigotry. While of course the truth is far more complicated, the Melungeon story clearly gives many average Turks *hope*, hope that their own nation can come to grips with its diversity. Such hope is vividly underscored in the handwritten letter of a thirteen-year-old Turkish girl who, because of the Melungeons, now sees herself as a cousin to her little Armenian classmate, and who wants identical Spice Girls music cassettes for the two of them. These are strange, unexpected spin-offs of an Appalachian people's journey of self-discovery, but all the better. While we Melungeons in the beginning saw the developing Turkish-Appalachian relationship as more self-serving—that is, giving us Melungeons something of emotional value—it has become increasingly clear that it is instead a quid-pro-quo transaction. And it is an exchange that, if properly understood and nurtured, can bear beneficial fruit for *all* Turks and Americans, whatever their ethnic or political or religious inclinations. That is one reason that I personally feel a commitment to seeing these links further developed.

The Magic of Denizli

Nowhere has this potential been more visibly demonstrated than in a village in southwestern Anatolia. In July 1999, I had the opportunity to address the Turkish and Central Asian Congress held in Denizli, Turkey. I remember in vivid detail my thoughts as I flew through an appropriately turquoise sky toward a rendevous with hundreds of Central Asian and Turkic people, from the Balkans and Turkey, to Azerbaijan and Mongolia. It was billed as a nonpolitical, nonnationalistic cultural event and afterwards I found myself in agreement that they had indeed succeeded in avoiding the traps of political or militaristic pan-Turanism (that is, pan-Turkism). The emphasis was purely on cultural and economic ties, with a palpable aura of excitement and anticipation present throughout the three-day event. I saw and sensed it, and others commented on how, as never before, all these people from all these different countries, had truly interacted as One People without infringing on individual nationhood. There was a mass pride in shared origins, and a sense that from Mongolia to Turkey—and maybe even to America—there was at long last a common-held pride of kinship. The central Asians were no different in their needs and dreams than the European Unionists, or the Pan-Arabists, or the Pan-Africanists. It also didn't take long for me to realize that in a way, and despite my own mixed background, much of me was also making its way "home." Despite my blue eyes and surname of Kennedy, I carried with me physically inseparable anthropological markers of long forgotten Asian and Mongolian ancestors. Central Asian shoveled incisors, a Mongolian "blue" spot at the base of my spine, an

enhanced external occipital protuberance, and recent personal and ancestral DNA sequencing irrefutably tying my immediate family to Siberia/
Mongolia (as well as other more "Ottoman" locales such as the Aegean
coastal areas, Cyprus, Palestine, Yemen, Lebanon, and even northern
India), confirming my genetic, if not cultural, "license" to be there. Like
the southern European Turks in attendance, my family, too, had its oral
traditions of "Turkish" ancestry (for example, my "Halls" were self-
described "Turks" and "Portuguese" in eighteenth-century eastern
Virginia, but became "English" upon arrival in southwestern Virginia in
the early 1800s). And my late-in-life diagnosis of familial Mediterranean
fever (1998) further entrenched me in the company of Turks, Armenians,
non-Ashkenazi Jews, and the Arab Druse. Later in the conference one
speaker mentioned the poetic Mongol adage meant to incorporate all Turkic and Mongol descendants into a broader family: "You left on horse-
back with slanted brown eyes, and you returned with blue eyes by plane."
In my case, a stunningly accurate parable.

Though many of earth's peoples could fit a similar migration and
reassimilation pattern, at that instant it did indeed strike a note with me.
It mattered little if my genes had come westward via the Mongol Hordes,
or eastward across the Bering Strait. All that mattered was that they had
come, and that I was here.

When my turn came to speak I took a moment and glanced out at the
large audience in front of me. The faces of the prototypical "Mongols"
blended like a river with the features of Russian-appearing Tartars, Jewish
Turks from Kazakistan, blond, blue-eyed "Turks" from the Balkans, and
even a few Christian Armenian businessmen who felt themselves to be
a part of the "Turkic World." I stole a glance at my traveling mate and
friend Frank Keel, a Choctaw-Chickasaw attorney and eastern director of
the Bureau of Indian Affairs, and for a moment found myself wondering
if perhaps *his* people were the ancestors of central Asians as opposed to
the other way around. Despite the longstanding academic dismissal of the
possibility, common sense would dictate that any human being could,
with a minimum of inventiveness, walk both east and west across the
Bering Strait. Either way, new DNA sequencing published by the
Smithsonian and other sources now demonstrates an undeniable genetic
relationship between central and even western Asians and some Native
American tribes. Neither Frank nor I would need a DNA analysis to
recognize the physical and cultural similarities as we later chatted in

depth with several central Asian shamans. We could just as easily have been in the American west, talking with our own indigenous people.

A *Quick History*

I spoke as efficiently as possible, providing a quick history of the Melungeons. I brought in all the ethnic groups that made us who we are. I told of our probable Jewish ancestors and our claims of Portuguese and Native American roots. I expounded on our African links and how, today, the original Melungeon gene pool has extended itself across America, making us all part and parcel of whatever an eighteenth-century Melungeon was. I drove home the point that the beauty of this story was not that a band of "pure-blooded" Turks had made its way to America centuries ago and survived intact, but instead that Ottoman and other central Asian peoples had made their way to the New World in a variety of ways and had become, over time, Americans. I told them of the Karachai and Kavkas silk workers that had accompanied the sixteenth-century Spanish to Cuba, Mexico, Florida, and the American Southwest. I told them of how almost certainly Sir Francis Drake in 1586 had abandoned a hundred or more "Turks" (to use Drake's own term, though he further describes them as Turks, Moors, Portuguese, and renegade Greeks who had converted to Islam) on Roanoke Island, North Carolina, in order to make room for the returning English colony of Ralph B. Layne. I informed them of the growing archival evidence that Turkish and Armenian artisans had formed a significant portion of the so-called "indentured-servant" population of seventeenth-century Jamestown, and that even their family names were extant in such records as *The Virginia Carolorum* (for example, Mehmet the Turk, Ahmad the Turk, Joseph the Armenian, Sayyan Turk, Tony Eastindian, and so on). I mentioned briefly that—directly from England itself—so-called Gypsies and other Ottoman peoples were sent as both settlers and servants, almost all bearing common English—and now Melungeon-related—surnames (for example, Adams, Adkins, Belcher, Clark, Greene, Hall, Mullins, Roberson, Sutherland, and so on). I presented the "new" evidence that Queen Elizabeth had brokered secret deals with the Ottomans and the king of Morocco to settle the New World together in order to shut out the Spanish and the French, and the probable ethnic ramifications of these cooperative agreements. I completed my quick tour of history with comments on Spain's major sixteenth-century settlements in South

Carolina, North Carolina, Georgia, and Tennessee. And how, coincidentally, they too were upended by the English in 1586, effectively cutting off hundreds of Spanish and Portuguese settlers at the foothills of the Appalachians. I stressed the equally important fact that many, if not most, of these settlers were "conversos"—Muslims and Jews who had converted to Christianity during the Inquisition. I offered theories on the origin of the term "Melungeon" itself, always associated with our people wherever they might have been. I explained that while present-day scholars point to the spelling as indicative of a French origin (from *melange*, "mixture"), that the earliest forms right up through the 1930s were invariably written as "malunjun" or "mahloonjun," and that it possibly was not the French who had given our people this name, but instead the English, who almost without doubt had picked it up from the Melungeons themselves (though they had come to resent the term, probably because of the legal ramifications of being Melungeon). I pointed out that, in fact, archival records indicate the seventeenth-century French referred to the Melungeons as "Moors." Though its origin remains unproved, the term is pronounced the same as both the Arabic *melun jinn* and the Turkish variation *melun can*, both phrases meaning "cursed soul." The term itself is merely the tip of a linguistic iceberg, with hundreds of Appalachian and related Native American words and even complete phrases having their seeming counterparts in Arabic, Turkish, and Central Asian dialects. Qualified linguists are now exploring these areas and time will tell us the degree, if any, of real connectivity.

Finally, I presented the published results of a 1990 gene-frequency analysis that showed (despite a lack of comparable Turkish genetic data) that 177 Melungeons were indeed related to populations in Portugal, Malta, Cyprus, North Africa, northern Iraq, and the Levant. As this book is going to press, more comprehensive DNA studies are underway that may strengthen the Melungeon claim of a Turkish and/or Mediterranean heritage (see below, chapter 4). In short, the preponderance of widespread oral tradition, supportive archival records, linguistics, physical phenotypes, and medical/genetics evidence seems, frankly, overwhelming. There are indeed tangible—and provable—cultural and genetic links between at least some Melungeons and Native Americans and their central Asian/Aegean Turkic-speaking counterparts halfway around the world. It is a true awakening and the illumination is growing.

The list of mutual interests and cooperation continues to grow. Here are but a few examples of the cooperative efforts that have been successfully undertaken.

•Wise, Virginia and Çeşme, Turkey won a major International Sister Cities Award in 1997. Much national attention here was focused on the event. When one understands that Wise, Virginia has a total population of 3,500 people, the magnitude of this award becomes apparent.

•The University of Virginia's College at Wise is now a sister institution with both Istanbul University and Dumlupinar University. At this writing, more than twenty-five Turkish students have attended UVaWise as exchange students, serving as wonderful ambassadors for Turkey. One student, Alihan Karakartal, presented the student address at the 2002 graduation ceremonies.

•Professor Mary O'Quinn of UVaWise participated in the Turkic World Women's Conference in Istanbul in May, 1999, and is completing a study comparing self-imagery between Appalachian Melungeon women and women of rural Anatolia.

•Professor Garrett Sheldon of UVaWise has published a book comparing the political philosophies of Mustafa Kemal Atatürk and Thomas Jefferson.

•A group of ten UVaWise officials, including Chancellor Jay Lemons, visited Istanbul University and Dumlupinar University in June 1999.

•Dozens of Wise County, Virginia school children have become pen pals with children in Çeşme, Turkey.

•The Melungeon Heritage Association, in conjunction with UVaWise's public radio station WISE-FM and East Tennessee State University's WETS-FM, assisted in the raising of approximately $75,000 for earthquake relief. The funds came almost exclusively from local people in an eight-county area in the heart of Appalachia.

•The late Turkish entertainer Baris Manco took an extraordinary interest in the Melungeon people, travelling to the United States in 1994 to produce several television programs and newspaper articles on our people.

•In 1998, on behalf of myself and others, I accepted the Fitz Turner Award for Civil Rights from the Virginia Education Association, in recognition of the groundbreaking interethnic-relations work represented by the diversity of the so-called "Melungeon Movement."

•The Melungeon Heritage Association (MHA) is now a full member of the Assembly of Turkish American Associations (ATAA).

•In 1998, on behalf of my people, I accepted the Distinguished Service Award from the ATAA in recognition of the cooperative efforts between our two peoples.

•Turkish delegations, cultural groups, and simply interested Turkish-Americans are always in attendance at the Melungeon Heritage Association's annual events (called "Unions"), generally drawing crowds in excess of 2,000, including Melungeon descendants, scholars, and interested media.

An *Irreversible* Movement

Whatever the final scholarly verdict may be on the origins of these so-called "mystery people," a seemingly irreversible association has developed between the various Turkic populations of the world and the Melungeons of Appalachia. This book is an exploration, as opposed to an explanation, of these developing relationships. Purely governmental leaders have been purposefully avoided, with the exception of Turkish Ambassador Faruk Loğoğlu. Major or sweeping political or social implications and interpretations are likewise not within the scope of this particular work (though these issues may well be explored in later publications). What we sought for this exploratory study were the genuine, heartfelt opinions and, frankly, emotions of those Americans, Turkish-Americans, and Turks living the relationship on a day-to-day basis.

By better understanding how bonds of kinship can develop between what on the surface may seem to be unlikely partners, we may all gain a keener insight into human interaction across, or in spite of, supposed national, cultural, and linguistic barriers. If lessons in friendship can be learned from the common folk of Appalachia and Anatolia, then why not learn them? And then take it a step further with the realization that no people on earth, however isolated or wretched, are beyond reach or hope. And that, furthermore, no people are too insignificant to matter on the world stage. We are Melungeons and we are Appalachians and we are Americans. We have a renewed pride and a regained sense of self. We have hope, and, perhaps most importantly, we most definitely matter.

September 2002

* | * | *

Suggested Reading List

Ball, Bonnie Sage. *The Melungeons: Their Origin and Kin*. Eighth edition. Haysi VA: B. S. Ball, 1984. First edition, 1969.

Bible, Jean Patterson. *Melungeons Yesterday and Today*. Jeffereson City TN: Bible, 1975 (printed for the author by East Tennessee Printing Co., Rogersville TN).

Bone, Patrick. *A Melungeon Winter*. A Silver Dagger Mystery. Johnson City TN: Overmountain Press, 2001.

Callahan, Jim. *Lest We Forget: The Melungeon Colony of Newman's Ridge*. Johnson City TN: Overmountain Press, 2000.

Elder, Pat Spurlock. *Melungeons: Examining An Appalachian Legend*. Blountville TN: Continuity Press, 1999.

Gallegos, Eloy J. *The Melungeons: The Pioneers of the Interior Southeastern United States, 1526–1997*. The Spanish Pioneers in United States History. Knoxville TN: Villagra Press, 1997. Knoxville: Tennessee Valley Press, 1997.

Goins, Jack Harold. *Melungeons and Other Pioneer Families*. Rogersville TN: self-published, 2000.

Hirschman, Elizabeth C. *The Melungeons: The Last Lost Tribe in America*. Macon GA: Mercer University Press, 2004.

Johnson, Mattie Ruth. *My Melungeon Heritage*. Johnson City TN: The Overmountain Press, 1997.

Kennedy, N. Brent, with Robyn Vaughan Kennedy. *The Melungeons: The Resurrection of a Proud People. An Untold Story of Ethnic Cleansing in*

America. Macon GA: Mercer University Press, 1994. Second, revised and corrected edition, 1997.

Kessler, John S., and Donald B. Ball. *North from the Mountains. A Folk History of the Carmel Melungeon Settlement, Highland County, Ohio*. Macon GA: Mercer University Press, 2001.

Langdon, Barbara Tracy. *The Melungeons: An Annotated Bibliography: References in Both Fiction and Nonfiction*. Woodville TX: Dogwood Press, 1998.

Loewen, James W. *Lies My Teacher Told Me: Everything Your American History Textbook Got Wrong*. (1) New York: New Press / Norton, 1994. (2) A Touchstone Book. New York: Simon & Schuster, 1996.

Marler, Don C. *Redbones of Louisiana*. Hemphill TX: Dogwood Press, 2003.

Matar, Nabil I. *Turks, Moors, and Englishmen in the Age of Discovery*. New York: Columbia University Press, 1999.

Mira, Manuel. *The Forgotten Portuguese: The Melungeons and Other Groups*. Portuguese Making of America: Early North-American History. Franklin NC: Portuguese-American Historical Research Foundation, 1998.

Naylor, Phyllis Reynolds. *Sang Spell*. A Jean Karl Book. New York: Atheneum Books for Young Readers, 1998.

Reed, Ishmael, editor. *Multi-America: Essays on Cultural Wars and Cultural Peace*. New York: Viking, 1997. New York: Penguin Books, 1998.

Rountree, Helen C. *Pocahontas's People: The Powhatan Indians of Virginia through Four Centuries*. The Civilization of the American Indian, volume 196. Norman OK: University of Oklahoma Press, 1990.

Stewart, Ethel G. *The Dene and Na-Dene Indian Migration—1233 A.D.: Escape from Genghis Khan to America*. Columbus GA: ISAC Press, 1991.

Stuart, Jesse. *Daughter of the Legend*. New edition, edited and with a preface by John H. Spurlock; introduction by Wilma Dykeman; afterword by N. Brent Kennedy. Ashland KY: Jesse Stuart Foundation, 1994, 1993. First edition: New York: McGraw-Hill, 1965.

Vande Brake, Katherine. *How They Shine: Melungeon Characters in the Fiction of Appalachia*. Macon GA: Mercer University Press, 2001.

Vardy Community Historical Society, DruAnna Overbay (secretary) et al. Introduction by Katie Hoffman Doman. *Windows on the Past: The Cultural Heritage of Vardy, Hancock County, Tennessee*. Sneedville TN: Vardy Community Historical Society, 2002.

Winkler, Wayne. *Walking toward the Sunset: The Melungeons*. Macon GA: Mercer University Press, 2003.

Suggested Websites

<http://freepages.genealogy.rootsweb.com/~rosadove/DeeDovey'sPage/racetc.htm>
<http://www.melungeons.com>

\<http://www.melungeon.org>
\<http://www.melungeonhealth.org>
\<http://appalachian_home.tripod.com/melungeon.htm>
\<http://www.angelfire.com/tn3/youngeagle>
\<http://www.geocities.com/mikenassau/definition.htm>
\<http://www.melungeon.info/links.htm>

Suggested Internet Articles

\<http://www.zwire.com/site/news.cfm?brd=1283>
\<http://www.wired.com/news/medtech/0,1286,53165,00.html>
\<http://www.bristolnews.com/front/MGBR6T02O2D.html>
\<http://www.zwire.com/site/news.cfm?newsid=4497579&BRD=1283&PAG
=461&dept_id=158544&rfi=6>
\<http://www.timesnews.net/index.cgi?CONTEXT=cat&BISKIT
=102367574410684&id=61418&category=54>
\<http://www.charlotte.com/mld/charlotte/news/3526955.htm>
\<http://www.wired.com/news/technology/0,1282,53383,00.html>
\<http://www.wired.com/news/technology/0,1282,53256,00.html>
\<http://www.zwire.com/site/news.cfm?newsid=4497579&BRD=1283&PAG
=461&dept_id=158544&rfi=6>
\<http://www.wired.com/news/technology/0,1282,53428,00.html>
\<http://www.wired.com/news/technology/0,1282,53440,00.html>
\<http://www.angelfire.com/tn3/youngeagle/MELUNGEON_or_MALENGIN.htm>
\<http://hometown.aol.com/vardyvalley/>
\<http://www.geocities.com/ourmelungeons/jgdef.html>

Suggested Early Anthropological Links
(via \<http://archiver.rootsweb.com>)

\<http://archiver.rootsweb.com/th/read/Melungeon/2003-02/1044396994>
\<http://archiver.rootsweb.com/th/read/Melungeon/2003-02/1044632579>
\<http://archiver.rootsweb.com/th/read/Melungeon/2003-02/1044884959>
\<http://archiver.rootsweb.com/th/read/Melungeon/2003-02/1044891979>
\<http://archiver.rootsweb.com/th/read/Melungeon/2003-03/1046623082>
\<http://archiver.rootsweb.com/th/read/Melungeon/2003-03/1046965132>

3

Interviews

(N.B.: With the exception of that of Colonel Carroll Goyne, all interviews were conducted prior to the release of the 2002 DNA study report.)

American Interviewees

- *Connie Clark*, past president, Melungeon Heritage Association (MHA), high school teacher, and a Melungeon descendant.
- *Carroll Goyne*, Melungeon researcher, retired military officer.
- *Frank Keel*, eastern director, Bureau of Indian Affairs, and a Choctaw-Chickasaw Indian.
- *Caynor Smith*, former mayor of Wise, Virginia, and a Melungeon descendant.
- *Wayne Winkler*, president, Melungeon Heritage Association, director and station manager of WETS (public radio), East Tennessee State University, and a Melungeon descendant.

* | * | *

o *Connie Clark*   Past president, Melungeon Heritage Association, Big Stone Gap, Virginia. Interviewed 30 May 2002.

1. *When did you first hear about Melungeons and what were your first impressions of these so-called "mystery people"?*

I first heard about Melungeons and the word "Melungeon" in the mid-seventies. There was an article in our local paper about a group of "mysterious people" living on High Knob. My soon-to-be husband brought the article for me to read. The theory of that time was they were a tri-isolate group living on the tops of mountains. I found the story fascinating and asked questions about them. They supposedly were a mixed group of whites, African Americans, and Native Americans. I questioned then if there could be no other mixes. All I can remember is I wanted to know more.

We traveled to Sneedville, Tennessee where an outdoor drama was supposed to be going on. We got there and found out that the drama *Walk unto the Sunset* was not playing anymore. I was disappointed.

I asked my soon-to-be husband what was peculiar about these people. He told me that they were dark-skinned, had ridges above their eyes, and had strange looking eyes. All I saw when I looked at them were the most wonderful blue eyes looking back at me from their dark faces. I thought most of them looked a lot like my cousins and ancestors.

2. When did you first believe that you were yourself of Melungeon heritage, and how did you feel about it?

I had read a few articles in the newspapers in the area and realized a person by the name of Brent Kennedy was going to speak on the topic of Melungeons in 1992. I had spent a year since my husband died looking into my ancestry. I had been told some years before that our family had some Native American heritage. I went to the talk at what was then Clinch Valley College of the University of Virginia [now the University of Virginia's College at Wise] at the Chapel of All Faiths. The chapel was full with standing room only. The speech was intriguing; it answered many of the questions that I had asked all of life. For example, questions were answered about our migration from North Carolina and how we could be Scots-Irish, German, English, and Native American. It also answered questions about anthropological markers, such as Asian eyefolds, shovel teeth, and the so-called "ramp knot" on the back of the head. I realized then that there was more of a mix than what my family knew or were willing to tell. I was wonderfully surprised and proud of the fact. I wanted to know more.

I called my mother from the college and told her about what I found out. She was not as happy about the information as I was and would not talk to me for about a month. But when we did talk, I realized she knew much more than she had ever shared with me before.

She had a little story she told me about the time her father walked past her when she was washing up for dinner. She was scrubbing up and all he said to her was, "I used to try to wash it off myself, but it doesn't come off." At that moment I knew she knew and she understood what I was telling her. No long silences were between us again. She told me as much as she knew about the dark-skinned ones in our family. And they happened to come from both sides who turned out to be the Mullinses.

3. *How would you define or describe Melungeons?*

I am going to answer this question with what the Melungeon Heritage Association, Inc. board of directors has researched and released on our web site at <http://www.melungeons.org>.

The Melungeons are a sizable mixed-ethnic population spread throughout the southeastern United States and into southern Ohio and Indiana. While the term "Melungeon" is most commonly applied to those group members living in eastern Kentucky, southwestern Virginia, eastern Tennessee, and southern West Virginia, related mixed-ancestry populations also include the Carmel Indians of southern Ohio, the Brown People of Kentucky, the Guineas of West Virginia, the We-Sorts of Maryland, the Nanticoke-Moors of Delaware, the Cubans and Portuguese of North Carolina, the Turks and Brass Ankles of South Carolina, and the Creoles and Redbones of Alabama, Mississippi, and Louisiana. Probable Native American kinship for the various groups includes the Algonquin tribes of eastern and central Virginia, as well as the Lumbees, Monacans, Saponi, Catawba, Cherokee, and Muskogee/Creek tribes of the deeper south. While each of the various subgroups possesses its own unique history and culture, historical and cultural evidence suggests a broad kinship between the groups and a probable common origin, through centuries of population dispersion and admixture have influenced the ethnic and social character of each of the separate populations. Regardless of the original ethnic and/or racial background of the first Melungeons, today we find Melungeon descendants among all mixed-ancestry groups, even some raised to think of themselves as "white" or Caucasian.

4. *How strong do you think the evidence is about Melungeons? What work remains to be done in the future to identify the origins?*

A growing body of evidence supports the now-centuries-old Melungeon claim to be of Portuguese, Turkish, Moorish, Arabic, and Jewish origin, mixed with Native Americans. Oral tradition, and cultural evidence seem to point toward a Mediterranean and Middle Eastern heritage among most of the Melungeon related peoples.

We need to collect more oral histories and family stories, and there needs to be more genealogies researched. There needs to be a team effort in research. By this I mean that people should be designated to do nothing but spend hours, days, months, and even years in research. We need to set up an institute that does nothing but research. In this research, of course, there would be travel. And along with that comes expenses. And then I really don't know if we will ever find the origins.

Because of the discrimination in the past and a desire to get "white" quicker, evidence may have been lost forever. I know that several families have had evidence destroyed when the Melungeon story started being renewed again that could help find the origins. Once destroyed we will never get it back.

5. *What is the significance of the Melungeon story in general?*

People may not be what they think they are. I invited Dr. Joe Smiddy [former chancellor of UVaWise and noted Appalachian political and cultural leader] to my classroom some years ago, and he told the students something that has stuck with me over those years. "You have to know where you come from to know where you are going." I've never forgot that.

Learning the differences in people can help the world in general. Having the knowledge of others can do nothing but strengthen the world and make it a better place for all of us.

6. *What is the personal significance to you?*

I see everyone in a different light. I have never thought I was a prejudiced person, but this knowledge I have received has been humbling to say the least. I am happy to know that I have ancestors that persevered so that I could be here today. If one gene had been different, I would not be here to enjoy the knowledge I have obtained from all of this.

7. *What do you believe will occur in the next 10 to 20 years?*

I hope more books will be written with evidence of our heritage. And I would like to see textbooks rewritten to include Melungeon materials. Traditionalists will disagree, but there is definitely enough evidence to prove we exist.

8. *What are the major obstacles, if any, to be overcome?*

Discrimination and prejudice.

9. *What impact, if any, do you see on the medical field, and particularly on the healthcare needs, of the Melungeon people that may derive from related research?*

This will and should turn the medical field around. Medical journals should start having articles appear about the diseases with the evidence given for such articles. Updates should be given periodically and new training courses for doctors should be started ASAP.

This will be a godsend for our people who have suffered unbearable pain for years.

10. *Do you personally know of any Melungeon people diagnosed with genetically based Mediterranean diseases (e.g., FMF, Thalassemia, Behçet's, Machado-Joseph, Tay-Sachs)?*

Yes, several.

11. *What would you say to physicians who do not recognize, properly diagnose, or treat members of the Melungeon community?*

First of all, most physicians are in denial. They are under the impression that all of us are of Scots-Irish ancestors. I would say that they need materials sent to them on the diseases, or, better yet, a seminar led by one of the doctors who is working with us. This way the leader would have a hands-on and face-to-face captive audience.

12. *What progress has been made in teaching Appalachian children, and others for that matter, about our diverse American heritage?*

I know that teachers in the state of Virginia have had exposure to this information on several occasions. There are training sessions every year on diversity throughout our state.

In my classroom I teach a unit on Melungeons. The students do a family tree, bring in pictures of ancestors, and discuss family. I know that many teachers, even in biology and science, have students research the diseases. By doing this students are beginning to learn about the symptoms, the names of the diseases, and treatments. Some students are finding that people in their families have these diseases. In history classes the teachers always spend some time with Melungeon theories.

13. *What is lacking in the teaching in the region about the story and its significance?*

I think that all teachers should teach about the Melungeons, but since it doesn't appear in the books and we have such pressure with the mandated areas we have to cover, we don't have the time to add on to what has to be done.

We need to have the opportunity to teach the children about diversity and mixed cultures. Until the subject of Melungeons is covered in the books or a supplement is added, I don't see teachers doing more than what they are doing now.

14. *What should be done in the next twenty years?*

I have hopes that there will be a greater emphasis placed on teaching diversity. The subject of Melungeons should be added to the books so that teachers have information in front of them that they can assign. I would like to see elective courses offered that deal with nothing but diversity.

15. *Please describe the basic nature and function of the Melungeon Heritage Association (MHA)?*

The Melungeon Heritage Association is a nonprofit organization. Our mission is to document, educate, and preserve the heritage and cultural legacy of mixed-ancestry peoples in or associated with the southern Appalachians. While our focus will be on those of Melungeon heritage, we will not restrict ourselves to honoring only this group. We firmly believe in the dignity of all such mixed ancestry groups of the southern Appalachians and commit to preserving and educating others about this rich heritage about racial harmony and diversity.

* | * | *

○ *Carroll H. Goyne, Jr.* Colonel, U.S. Air Force (retired). Shreveport, Louisiana. Interviewed July 2002.

1. *When did you first hear about the Melungeons and what were your first impressions of these so-called "mystery people"?*

I first heard about the Melungeons in July 1990, when reading a paper written by Dr. Virginia Easley DeMarce entitled "A Genealogical Look at Melungeons (with reference to some other American Triracial Isolates)." I was intrigued by Dr. DeMarce's paper, and was happy to become involved in Melungeon research when so invited in 1996.

2. *When did you first believe that you were yourself of Melungeon heritage, and how did you feel?*

I have conducted genealogical research on many of my family lines for about twenty years, and have found no evidence that suggests I may have Melungeon heritage. All of my immigrant ancestors, that I have identified, came to America from the British Isles. I am still open to the possibility that I may have a Melungeon "grandmother" out there somewhere.

3. *How would you define or describe "Melungeons"?*

I doubt if anyone can "define" Melungeons, except to say that they are a people of mixed ancestry. Some researchers have defined Melungeons in sociological terms, rather than in ethnic terms. The physical appearance of some Melungeon descendants, and photographs of older-generation Melungeons, reveals them to be a people of Mediterranean appearance, with varying degrees of light-to-dark skin.

4. How strong do you think the evidence is about Melungeons? What work remains to be done in further identifying their origins?

Probably, each Melungeon family had a different heritage. For example: after limited genealogical research on Vardeman Collins, we find that he had a mixed heritage of English, Irish, Swedish, Welsh, and perhaps Melungeon. If Vardeman Collins had Melungeon ancestry, I would estimate that his Melungeon ancestor married into his male Collins line one or two generations prior to a Collins-Vardeman marriage.

A new set of questions has been generated by the results of the Melungeon DNA project. A major finding of the project was that a vast majority (90%) of Melungeon people tested had neither American Indian nor African ancestry. This comes as a surprise, for I had thought the American Indian percentage would be much higher than five percent, because late eighteenth- and early nineteenth-century Melungeons lived among or near the Cherokee Indians.

An early Basque presence in North America has been largely ignored. Archeological and linguistical evidence proves that Basque people were in North America from a very early time, possibly before the time of Christ. Evidence is that Basque fishing fleets had found the Grand Banks off Newfoundland before 1500. Algonquian Indians from as far away as the Appalachian Mountains traded with them on Isle aux Basque in the St. Lawrence River. Notarial records in the Basque ports of southwestern France list some of the trade goods found in Algonquian archeological sites on Isle aux Basque. Some Algonquian Indians of the Great Lakes region, including James Bay, spoke a Basque dialect, and used the ancient Basque syllabary. Numerous Basque inscriptions have been found in the Susquehanna River valley and in eastern Tennessee. Could the Basque be the "Portagees" of Melungeon legend?

For the future, I would recommend that additional genealogical and genetics research be conducted on selected Melungeon families.

5. What is the significance of the Melungeon story in general?

As this nation matured, and the population increased and the more desirable lands were taken up, people who were viewed as "different" came to be seen as an inconvenience to the dominant race. Those who felt threatened moved to the frontiers, usually in groups for protection. The mountains of the east were a refuge for them for a time. After independence, some Melungeon families moved into the narrow "free strip" created when the survey parties of North Carolina and Virginia could not agree upon the line to be surveyed for a state boundary west of the Blue Ridge. Each state surveyed its own line, creating a "free strip" of some eight miles in width extending from the Blue Ridge to Cumberland Gap. For several years, this was a land beyond the law and without taxes, therefore a territory attractive to many people. The "free strip" between Louisiana and Texas also attracted many people for the same reasons. Some of the names in the Louisiana-Texas "free strip" can be connected with Melungeon and Red Bone names in the eastern part of the country. The Melungeon story teaches us that prejudice and persecution have no place in a free society. All persons ought to have equal rights, and receive equal treatment in this great land.

6. *What is the personal significance to you?*

Melungeon research has afforded me an opportunity to study history from a different perspective. I have been delighted with the many tangential paths I have explored. I have learned that written history sometimes reflects the bias of the author and of his nationality. Of great significance to me was the realization that American history did not begin with Columbus.

7. *What do you believe will occur in the next ten to twenty years?*

Hopefully, research will be conducted in the Ottoman Archives to determine the fate of the some 10,000 Turks who were taken prisoner by the "allies" at the Battle of Lepanto in 1571. Spain claimed half of these prisoners, since she contributed half of the ships and money. There is good evidence that the Spanish transported some of these Turks to the New World. The English returned 100, or more, from the Americas to their homeland in 1586–1587. Their account of events might shed some light on the fate of the others. Such information could provide important clues to the Turkic origins of the Melungeons.

The new science of "Genetic Genealogy" (utilizing DNA sequencing to prove/disprove family and/or ehtnic relationships) might better define some Melungeon family lines.

8. *What are the major obstacles, if any, to be overcome?*

Many Melungeon researchers are working independently. Hopefully, the planned Melungeon Center will become a Melungeon archives. If all persons involved in Melungeon research will contribute copies of their research to this facility, the resultant cooperative research effort will produce results much sooner than persons working independently.

9. *What impact, if any, do you see on the medical field, and particularly on the healthcare needs of the Melungeon people that may derive from related research?*

Melungeons can only benefit from more medical research on rare genetic diseases. The medical profession should understand that some of these diseases are not so rare among the Melungeons. Since Melungeon descendants are widespread in this country, the knowledge for treating these diseases should also be widespread.

10. *Do you personally know of any Melungeon people diagnosed with a genetically based Mediterranean disease (e.g., FMF, thalassemia, Behçet's, Machado-Joseph, Tay-Sachs)?*

One person I know has FMF.

11. *What would you say to physicians who do not recognize, properly diagnose, or treat members of the Melungeon community?*

I would recommend to those doctors that they become better educated on the rare genetic diseases. Otherwise, as a patient, I would seek a doctor who could properly treat me. It might be helpful if literature on these rare diseases was distributed to the medical profession across the country. Medical schools should include study of these rare genetic diseases in their curriculum.

12. *What progress had been made in teaching Appalachian children, and others for that matter, about our diverse American heritage? What is lacking in the teaching in the region about the story and its significance?*

N/A

13. *What should be done over the next twenty years?*

A Melungeon Center is a good idea. It ought to be easily accessible by airline and highway. Research of all types is called for. A coordinated research effort is needed. I would recommend added emphasis on genealogical research.

14. *Are there other Melungeon associations or organizations?*

To my knowledge, the only other organization interested in Melungeon research is the Gowen Research Foundation based in Lubbock, Texas.

15. *Do you believe there is an Ottoman and/or Turkic connection to the Melungeon people?*

Some Turks were aboard Sir Francis Drake's ships when he removed the Ralph Lane colony from Roanoke Island in 1586. Evidently, Drake had freed the Turks from the Spanish in Cartagena and/or Santo Domingo. Evidence suggests that none of these Turks were left on Roanoke Island, but were returned to England. There is evidence in English archival records that the Queen's Privy Council sought to return 100 or more Turks to their homeland. I believe there is a Turkic connection to the Melungeons, but I do not know where it occurred. There is evidence that some Turkic people were present in the Virginia Colony during the seventeenth century.

16. *You've been to Turkey numerous times. How does it resonate with your own heritage and culture?*

I have visited Turkey on four occasions, and have met Turks on all levels of the socioeconomic scale. I have found the Turks to be a warm and generous people, and they have a special place in their hearts for Americans. When I thanked a highly placed person in academia for treating me like a Turk, he said, "You are a Turk, an honorary one in any case." He then proceeded to invite my wife and me to join him and his wife at Friday prayer service at the Blue Mosque in Istanbul. I told him that I was not Muslim. He said he knew that I was Christian, but that didn't matter. What more can I say? I feel very much at home among the Turks.

17. *As your parting words, what would you like to tell the world about Melungeons?*

A solution to the Melungeon "mystery" may well cause portions of history to be rewritten. We have found that there are pieces of evidence that do not fit into the popular version of history. They may be Melungeon related, or they may not be. In any case, the true Melungeon story is just beginning to unfold. It is a story that needs to be told in truth and in its entirety.

* | * | *

o   *Frank Keel*   Eastern director, Bureau of Indian Affairs (BIA), Washington, D.C. and Nashville, Tennessee. Written interview: 6 March 2002.

1. *When did you first become interested in the possible connections between Ottoman-Turkic peoples and the Melungeons and some Native American tribes?*

A few years ago I renewed my acquaintance with Professor Türker Özdoğan. He and I had lived in the same dormitory at the George Washington University, in Washington, D.C. many years ago. He and I were both graduate students there at the time.

He informed me of his discovery of definite linguistic similarities between languages of the Athabascan tribes in North America and the Turkish language. He had also done some earlier research into similarities in textile designs in Navajo rugs and Turkish kilim rugs. He also mentioned the Melungeon/Turkish work that he had learned about. Having an abiding interest in American Indian culture and history, especially pre-Columbian, my interest was sparked.

2. *Overall, how strong do you think the evidence of the connection is at present?*

At this time, I am aware of only one anthropologist who has shown any interest in such a connection. She is Dr. Ethel G. Stewart, author of *The Dene and Na-Dene Indian Migration 1233 A.D.*, with the subtitle *Escape from Genghis Khan to America.*

I am acquainted with several anthropologists who specialize in American Indians. Most of them have shown no interest in a larger connection between American Indians and peoples outside the Western Hemisphere. However, most will admit that the Bering Strait theory doesn't explain the variety of cultures and languages among the native peoples of the Americas. Thus, I would say there is enough preliminary information to raise interesting questions. I hope that some open-minded contemporary scholars will enter this arena.

3. *What evidence do you think is the strongest? The weakest? Why?*

I think that Dr. Stewart's efforts offer much food for thought. The linguistic connection noted by Professor Özdoğan would seem to offer fertile ground for further work by interested scholars. Although I have heard of some serious students of the American native peoples who have found linguistic connections or artifacts relating to Middle Eastern or northern European peoples, those efforts have failed, for whatever reason, to generate widespread interest within the U.S. archaeological/anthropological community.

Unfortunately, most of the elders or other keepers of traditions who would be ready sources of tribal historical/cultural information have already died off or are at extremely advanced ages. That would force new scholars to work with already existing studies, to focus on "hard" evidence such as artifacts, or to use other data such as DNA, which appears to hold great promise in this field. (Of course, there is a risk that the issue of racism could arise among critics of this line of study.)

4. *Why do you think there was early resistance among some scholars to the idea that Melungeons might have Middle Eastern or Mediterranean heritage?*

By dint of their training, most archaeologists and anthropologists that I know are relatively closed-minded when it comes to new points of view. Or, they often have tunnel vision and simply don't want to look at information, which has been developed outside of their own discipline. Like a lot of people, they are simply resistant to change.

5. *Have you been surprised that the Melungeons have not sought federal recognition as Native Americans, even though they embrace at least a partial Native American heritage?*

No, I am not surprised. Possessing some American Indian heritage, like many Americans do, is not sufficient to warrant federal recognition as a tribe or even as a tribal citizen in most cases.

6. *Do any Native American tribes, or tribal representatives, have a connection with—or interest in—the Turkic World Research Foundation, or other Turkish organizations?*

To my knowledge no federally recognized tribes have a formal connection with the Turkic World Research Foundation. I am unaware of any tribal connections with any other Turkish organizations. However, several tribes that I have talked with have expressed an interest upon being informed of the Foundation and its interest in American Indians.

7. *You've visited Turkey twice, meeting both average Turks and university professors. You've also met with Turkic and Central Asian shamans. What was your experience like?*

My experience in meeting with Turks has been overwhelmingly positive. The country was beautiful and the people were extremely hospitable and friendly. (I also loved the food!) I have met Central Asians in Russia as well as in Turkey and, again, the experience was extremely positive.

8. *Did you sense any possibility of cultural and/or genetic connections to Turks and other Ottoman peoples (e.g., Berbers, Arabs, Gypsies, Jews)?*

Although I did encounter persons who bore a strong resemblance to some of my relatives, I was not able to learn enough about their cultures to form an opinion as to possible cultural or genetic connections.

I would love to see a dialogue develop between American Indians and the Turkic ethnic groups.

9. *How do the Turkish people view Native Americans?*

Like many people throughout the world, the Turks view American Indians with much curiosity and much sympathy. Much curiosity, because no one really knows where all the American

Indians originated, and much sympathy, because of the tragedy of Indian/Non-Indian relations in the history of the Americas.

10. *You've participated in the Melungeon Heritage Festival in Wise, Virginia, where Melungeons and Turks have explored their possible connections. What was your impression of that event and how were you greeted as both a Choctaw and a representative of the BIA?*

I was honored to have been invited to the Festival. Like American Indians, Melungeons have been subjected to many cruelties and social inequities because of the perceptions and misperceptions of their non-Melungeon neighbors. I am very happy that they are exploring their heritage and want to find the truth of their origins, whatever it may be. Given their past history, I recognize the courage and determination required for such an undertaking. I wish them success in that exploration and strongly hope that it results in their gaining their rightful place in U.S. society.

I felt that I was well received both as an American Indian and as a government official. I met many interesting people there. It was a pleasure visiting with them.

* | * | *

o   *Caynor Smith* Mayor of Wise, Virginia, sister city to Çeşme, Turkey. Date of interview: 5 September 2000.

1. *When did you first hear about Melungeons and what were your first impressions of these so-called "mystery people"?*

I first heard of Melungeons when I was a young boy. I just thought they were a group of people who lived in southwest Virginia and eastern Kentucky.

2. *When did you first believe that you were yourself of Melungeon heritage, and how did you feel about it?*

I never really thought about myself having Melungeon heritage until I read Brent Kennedy's first book and soon thereafter had the opportunity to travel to Turkey as mayor of the town of Wise. I found it amazing and interesting to find that my heritage could be linked to missing Turkish sailors.

3. *How would you define or describe "Melungeons"?*

I would say Melungeons are a group of people who have married into different cultures.

4. *How strong do you think the evidence is about Melungeons? What work remains to be done in further identifying the origins?*

I think it is extremely strong based on Brent Kennedy's research. To further identify the origins I feel the public will need to be educated more and become more willing to share their personal stories.

5. *What is the significance of the Melungeon story in general?*

It is like finding the missing piece of a puzzle from our heritage. It makes sense and answers questions we have had for years. It allows these questions to be answered with a sense of pride and an added level of importance to our beginnings.

6. *What is the personal significance to you?*

For me personally, to know that hundreds of years ago Turkish sailors left their homeland and came to our country and many years later their children were able to return home. I was even more excited to be the first elected official to return home as one of these children. This is something that will influence me for the rest of my life.

7. *What do you believe will occur in the next ten to twenty years?*

My vision would be to expand our cultural and economic exchange not only between our sister cities and countries but also between cultures.

8. *What are the major obstacles, if any, to be overcome?*

Educating our people, erasing negative stereotypes, and increasing the desire to open our community to recognize these other cultures.

9. *What progress had been made in teaching Appalachian children, and others for that matter, about our diverse Amercian heritage? What is lacking in the teaching in the region about the story and its significance?*

If our students must learn about African American heritage, Native American heritage, etc. in our public schools, as evidenced in textbooks and nationally recognized holidays, then perhaps it's time to treat the Melungeon heritage with equal significance.

10. *What should be done over the next twenty years?*

There should be literature available to our children that is age appropriate to teach of this heritage, and other steps should be taken for public awareness.

11. *Do you believe there is an Ottoman and/or Turkic connection to the Melungeon people?*

Absolutely!

12. *How strong is the evidence for this connection?*

I feel it is very strong.

13. *You've been to Turkey. How does it resonate with your own heritage and culture?*

All people are the same . . . only governments and traditions seem to be different. The thing that sticks out the most was the strong sense of family.

14. *As your parting words, what would you like to tell the world about Melungeons?*

Melungeons are as diverse a people as any Americans. They have strong values, a unique culture, hands which have produced labor and hands which they will lovingly extend to others in friendship. Melungeons have strong and giving hearts and should now be known as the people with happy souls.

* | * | *

o   *Wayne Winkler*   President, Melungeon Heritage Association, and
                             director, WETS (public radio), East Tennessee
                             State University, Johnson City, Tennessee.
                             Interview conducted Friday, 8 February 2001.

1. *When did you first hear about Melungeons and what were your first
impressions of these so-called "mystery people"?*

I was twelve years old when I first learned of the Melungeons.
My dad came from Hancock County, so we went there to visit family
several times a year. This was in 1968, and I saw a copy of the
Hancock County Post that was full of articles about the Melungeons,
particularly about the outdoor drama that was being organized. I
thought it sounded pretty interesting, and immediately I thought of
several people I knew or had seen around Hancock County that
certainly looked like the description of Melungeons—plus I knew a
lot of people named Collins, Mullins, Gibson, etc.

2. *When did you first believe that you were yourself of Melungeon
heritage, and how did you feel about it?*

I knew that my father's father was Indian—my dad's whole
family looked very Indian, and I assumed that was our ethnic
heritage. When I asked my family about these Melungeons, nobody
seemed to want to talk about it, and my mother told me that my
dad's mother (who was still living) was a Melungeon.

I thought it was pretty cool. I had always known that I was a
white/Indian mix, and now I could include black as well. I grew up
around a lot of black people, and James Brown (one of my heroes)
had just released "Say It Loud, I'm Black and I'm Proud," so I was
glad because the song now included me. I realized, though, that not
everyone felt that way. Fortunately my mom and dad didn't have a
problem with it—I guess my mom wouldn't have married my dad if
she had a problem. Dad always had a lot of black friends, and he was
so dark they always teased him about being "one of them." I guess
it was more true than they realized.

3. *How would you define or describe "Melungeons"?*

The first definition of Melungeon I ever heard still sounds valid to me today, and that was a mix of black, white, and Indian. Whether the white component was English, Portuguese, Turkish, or whatever, whether the black component was Moorish or American slaves or freedmen, or whether the Indian was Cherokee, Saponi, or whatever, that original definition is still valid. Even if it were to be shown—as some people would like—that there was no African ancestry in the Melungeons, they were still considered part black by the neighboring whites, and were treated as such.

A lot of people today are using "Melungeon" as a generic term for *all* triracial people, and that's inaccurate. There are many triracial groups, though not all of them want to be considered as such. To use "Melungeon" as a generic term to describe them is to cheat them out of their own heritage. There needs to be a good generic term. Actually, I think "triracial" is a good generic term, but again, some individuals and groups object to the notion that they have African ancestry, so I doubt that will ever catch on widely. That's not necessarily due to racism; a lot of these groups are struggling with the federal government for recognition as Indian tribes, and a "triracial" designation tends to give the government an excuse not to grant that recognition. Still, I don't think people of Lumbee or Brass Ankle ancestry should be called "Melungeon" as a generic term; their ancestors were never called that. The only people who were called "Melungeon" 100 years ago were those who lived in or near Hancock County, Tennessee—including Lee, Scott, and Wise Counties in southwest Virginia. There was a community called "Melungeon" in Graysville, Tennessee, and scattered communities in southeastern Kentucky. Historically, these were the Melungeons. However, there are family connections with the "Carmel Indians" of Highland County, Ohio. These folks were never called "Melungeon" until very recently, but they were definitely our kinfolk. There are probably genetic connections between the Melungeons of Hancock County and other groups around the country, so I wouldn't make that definition too restrictive. Also, the term "Melungeon" had socioeconomic over-tones as well. Wealthy folks didn't get called "Melungeon," no matter who their families were. Obviously, "Melungeon" is not a precise term; it had a lot to do with who was saying it, and who they were saying it about.

4. *How strong do you think the evidence is about Melungeons? What work remains to be done in further identifying the origins?*

I've been researching the historical evidence, and it's pretty vague. However, in the last few years, bits of historical evidence have shown up. We now know that the term "Melungeon" was used as early as 1813, in the church minutes of Stony Creek Baptist Church in Scott County, Virginia. Perhaps someday an even earlier reference will be unearthed, and the time and place of that reference will tell us a lot. The biological evidence is fairly thin at the moment. Pollitzer and Brown's 1969 blood study, and Guthrie's 1990 reexamination of that data, give us a lot of information about the origins of the Melungeons, but we can't know how representative their samples were of the entire population. [See in supplemental materials below, "DNA Study Answers and Raises Questions about the Melungeons."] Dr. Kevin Jones's DNA study will give us a lot of information about the origin of the Melungeons, but there will still be work for historians and others to do in order to fill out that information. The DNA study might tell us where the genes came from, but not how those genes got to Hancock County.

5. *What is the significance of the Melungeon story in general?*

The Melungeons have taken an epithet and turned it into a badge of honor. I never heard of Melungeons before 1968 because no one used that term, at least not in front of me. That's because the word had such a negative connotation, and to call a man a Melungeon was to insult him. By about 1970, though, a lot of folks in Hancock County and elsewhere started identifying themselves as Melungeons, and they used the term with pride. Of course, that feeling wasn't universal, and still isn't; a lot of people still resist acknowledging that heritage. The Melungeons are just the tip of the iceberg, so to speak, of the multiracial, multiethnic people who have been a part of America's history from the very beginning. Still today, a lot of people—particularly in government—think only in terms of black and white. There are a lot of us brown people here, and we've always been here; we've just been forced to choose to be identified as either black or white. The publicity about Melungeons in the last decade has shown that racial lines have always been blurred in this country, and a lot of so-called "white" people are discovering that some of their ancestors weren't white. It has changed their perspective on issues of race and ethnicity.

6. *What is the personal significance to you?*

I have always resented the idea that I had to choose to identify as one race or another. I'm not a big fan of the concept of race; I prefer to think in terms of ethnicity, of culture and heritage. Anthropologists have now abandoned the whole concept of "race" in favor of ethnicity, and I think that's a healthy thing. The Melungeons are a practical example of the blurring of racial lines and boundaries, and for me, that's a comfortable thing. I can identify myself as Melungeon, and let that term cover the whole gamut of ethnicity that is in my background. Of course, I still have to explain to a lot of people just what a Melungeon is, but as time goes on, more people will understand that Americans have always had a diverse background. I heard someone on television talking about the children of "interracial" marriages today, and how they're having to choose to identify with one or the other parent's ethnic background. That's wrong; we should all be able to acknowledge and celebrate our own diversity of background.

7. *What do you believe will occur in the next ten to twenty years?*

I think a lot of other multiracial, multiethnic people will "come out of the closet," so to speak, and acknowledge and celebrate their diverse backgrounds. Perhaps when my daughter is grown, it won't be a big deal anymore; race will be an obsolete concept not just in science, but in society as well. Maybe I'm just dreaming—America has always been a race-obsessed county—but it's something to hope for, something to work toward.

8. *What are the major obstacles, if any, to be overcome?*

Not all the triracial or multiracial groups are as comfortable in celebrating their diversity as the Melungeons have been. The Melungeons were the subject of a novel by Jesse Stuart, and an outdoor drama by Kermit Hunter, both of which cast them in a positive light. Your book [Kennedy's *The Melungeons*] has also helped a lot of folks learn of and accept their diverse ethnic heritages.

Not everyone has been so fortunate. Some of the triracial groups have been struggling for recognition as Indians, and are not very open to accepting or acknowledging their diversity. Like any good American, I blame the government for this, at least in large part. The government says, in essence, "If your people aren't 'pure' Indian—meaning unmixed with blacks—you will not be recognized as Indians." This has forced them into rejecting much of their respective heritages, which is yet another form of cultural genocide. People are still forced to choose an ethnic identity, and that choice seems to be subject to government approval.

9. What impact, of any, do you see on the medical field, and particularly on the healthcare needs, of the Melungeon people that may derive from related research?

Well, you're [Kennedy] a perfect example. How long did it take the doctors to figure out that this "white" guy from Appalachia might have a medical condition usually found in Mediterranean or Middle Eastern people? As more physicians learn of the Melungeons and others like us, they will be less likely to assume that the ethnic background of a particular patient might not be what either the doctor or the patient assumes it is.

10. Do you personally know of any Melungeon people diagnosed with genetically based Mediterranean diseases (e.g., FMF, thalassemia, Behçet's, Machado-Joseph, Tay-Sachs)?

Only since I came to know you [Kennedy] and a few others in recent years. I never heard of any of those diseases among my family members or others in Hancock County when I was younger. Of course, they might well have had those diseases, but nobody thought to check. It could be that some of these folks had been misdiagnosed.

11. What would you say to physicians who do not recognize, properly diagnose, or treat members of the Melungeon community?

I'd say that they need to learn a bit of American history and not judge by appearances. A lot of "white" people and "black" people have diverse backgrounds, often without knowing it. Doctors shouldn't rule out possibilities just because the patient "looks white."

12. *What progress had been made in teaching Appalachian children, and others for that matter, about our diverse American heritage? What is lacking in the teaching in the region about the story and its significance?*

I think educators are just now starting to pick up on the idea that there is a much greater ethnic diversity among Americans—particularly "Scots-Irish" Appalachians—than they had previously thought. I know of a few teachers who are beginning to incorporate that into their lessons. We still have a very long way to go, but we have to remember that until a few years ago, few people had ever heard of the Melungeons or similar groups. I used to write school papers on the Melungeons, and I always got an "A" simply because the teachers had never heard of us before. As more educators become aware of this story, I think it will be reflected in their lessons.

13. *What should be done over the next twenty years?*

We need to establish, as much as possible, who we are and where we came from. There is a lot of controversy among researchers at present, and I'd like to see us come to a general consensus that can be supported by facts. Then we need to document our history as much as possible. Already, the "Melungeon community," even in Hancock County, is almost a thing of the past. Outsiders don't call us Melungeons anymore; the only way they know we *are* Melungeons is if we tell them. We don't exist as a people the way we did a hundred years ago, but we still exist as individuals, as families, and in that sense there are more of us now than ever before. We need to establish our place in the American history books.

14. *Please describe the basic nature and function of the Melungeon Heritage Association?*

The MHA was established to help promote and disseminate research on our people, and to give our people an institutional voice, which we've never had. Not all of us agree on who we are or where we came from; we all have our own theories and opinions. But we are all motivated, I think, by the desire to establish the Melungeons as a part of American history and American society. When I first met my wife, she asked about my ethnicity, and I told her "Melungeon." It was as if I had said "leprechaun"; to her, Melungeons were just an

Appalachian folktale. Now she's the wife and mother of Melungeons, and she knows we really do exist. The MHA wants the whole world to know we exist, and the MHA is going to be a big part of that educational process.

15. *Are there other Melungeon associations or organizations?*

There are a couple of organizations that I know of, in Atlanta and in Pittsburgh, but I don't know how well organized or how active they are. There are also two or three Melungeon e-mail groups on the Internet.

16. *What is the future of these organizations? How will they grow and change over the next decade, if at all?*

I'd like to see us all working together. That's not to say I think the MHA should absorb them all, but we should be in contact and work together when we can. During the civil rights era, there were several black organizations, including the NAACP, the Southern Christian Leadership Conference, the Congress of Racial Equality, and so on. These groups did not have identical views or priorities, but they were all working toward pretty much the same goals. I hope we will all be able to find common goals that we can all work toward.

17. *Do you believe there is an Ottoman and/or Turkic connection to the Melungeon people?*

I have to say that, at this point, I don't know. I'd like to think there is.

18. *How strong is the evidence for this connection?*

There is a lot of circumstantial evidence, and the connection is certainly possible. There were numerous opportunities for Ottoman and/or Turkish people to mingle with people on the North American continent. I hope further research can be done, both in America and in Turkey.

19. *You've been to Turkey numerous times. How does it resonate with your own heritage and culture?*

My visits to Turkey are the reason I hope there is a connection. My first day in Ankara, I walked around the city by myself—didn't understand a word anyone was saying, but somehow I felt pretty much at ease and at home. The people sure looked like my relatives! And the food! Turkish bread by itself is reason enough to want to be kin with them. As I got to know more Turkish people, the feeling of kinship grew even stronger. That's not evidence of a connection, of course; the Turks are warm, wonderful people who would make anyone feel welcome. Despite the different language, culture, and religious heritage, I felt an indescribable connection with the Turks. If research proves there is no connection between Melungeons and Turks, I would still want to return, and for myself, there is a connection that will always be there.

20. *As your parting words, what would you like to tell the world about Melungeons?*

First of all, that we exist; we're not some Appalachian fairy tale.

Secondly, that no matter how "diluted" our Melungeon heritage has become through mixing with European and African genes, we still retain a certain mysterious "something" that makes us Melungeons, a look or an aura that I've seen in both "white" and "black" people who share our heritage. And finally, I want to say that our story matters, that we represent an important part of the history and heritage of America.

* | * | *

Turkish and Turkish-American Interviewees

- *Oya Bain*. Regional vice president, Assembly of Turkish American Associations.
- *Tolga Çubukçu*. Past president, Assembly of Turkish American Associations.
- *Osman Faruk Loğoğlu*. Ambassador to the United States, Republic of Turkey.
- *Nur Serter*. Vice rector and professor of Economics, Istanbul University.
- *Türker Özdoğan*. Professor at George Washington University, Washington, D.C.
- *Hayri Ulgen*. Dean of the faculty of Business and Economics, Istanbul University.
- *Turan Yazgan*. Professor of Economics and president of the Turkish World Research Foundation.

* | * | *

○ *Oya Bain*   Regional vice president of the Assembly of Turkish American Associations (ATAA), Washington, D.C. Interviewed 10 February 2002.

1. *Were you born in the U.S. or did you immigrate here? If the latter, why did you come?*

I came to U.S. in 1960 to do graduate work in Biochemistry on a Fulbright Scholarship. I come from a well-established middle-class family in Turkey and had a relatively privileged upbringing in Istanbul (private schools, etc.). When I first came to U.S. in 1960, I had no plans to stay in the U.S.

2. *Why have you stayed?*

I married an American. I was also very impressed with the U.S. The job opportunities, the potential to grow more, freedom from old and sometimes irrational rules back at home, warmth of people— these were some of the factors which attracted me to the U.S.

3. *Have you become a U.S. citizen? If so, why?*

Yes, because I wanted to integrate into the American system and specifically participate fully in community activities and election process.

4. *What do you find positive in your experience as a Turkish-American in the U.S.? Negative? Any discrimination toward you or your family?*

My experience—I came to U.S. in 1960—has been nothing but positive in mainstream U.S. I did not see any discrimination in workplace or in private life. However, the negative propaganda against Turkey and the Turks, coming from the ethnic groups such as Greeks, Armenians, and now the Kurds made an impact. I felt very offended and wronged by the unfair and frequently baseless accusations in the media and in the U.S. Congress. Unfortunately, the political system allows for the legislators to be manipulated by militant ethnic groups, resulting in discriminatory resolutions and educational material against the Turks. Over the years, my sense of harrassment and frustration increased considerably.

5. *What would you most like to change in the Turkish-American relationship? Why? How would you change it?*

More than anything else, I would like to negate and neutralize the virulent anti-Turkish activities of militant ethnic lobbies which are aimed to create a poor image of Turks in the mainstream U.S. In parallel, I would like to work on educational and legislative projects that would promote the Turks and the strong alliance with the U.S.

6. *When did you first hear that some Native American tribes might have Turkic (Central Asian) roots?*

Approximately ten years ago through the efforts of Professor Türker Özdoğan (George Washington University).

7. *What did you think or feel about this possibility? Have you read/heard much about this? How strong/weak do you think the evidence is for such connections?*

At first, I thought it was farfetched, but as I read more about it, I felt there is plenty of evidence. Still, I am not very well informed on this subject as I would like to be.

8. *If true, how significant is this relationship (or how significant can it become) for Turks, Turkish-Americans, and Native Americans?*

I think it is very significant for the Turks. For decades Turks were considered the peoples confined to Anatolia and not much more, by Europe and U.S. The relationship between Central Asian Turks and Native Americans of the American continent broadens the scope of Turkic peoples to a huge geographical area and to a large variety of cultures. It brings a fascinating historical and anthropological perspective to the Turkish past.

9. *When did you first hear that the Melungeons might have connections to Ottoman period Turks and other Ottoman subjects?*

Approximately ten years ago, again through the efforts of Professor Özdoğan.

10. *What did you think or feel about this possibility? Have you read/heard much about this? How strong/weak do you think the evidence is for such connections?*

I feel strongly about this possibility as I read more about it. The evidence appears to be quite strong. DNA analysis results would be of great interest and would provide more definitive evidence.

11. *If true, how significant is this relationship (or how significant can it become) for Turks, Turkish-Americans, and Melungeon-Americans?*

Very significant. Culturally and historically, the relationship would provide a wealth of information to the American public. Also, the Turkish Americans and Melungeons can combine their voting powers and work together in legislative and social areas.

12. *What is the place of Turkish-Americans? Should they emphasize their "Turkishness" or simply become absorbed into the so-called American "melting pot"?*

Turkish Americans should integrate into the U.S. society, be more active in the community and legislative issues, but not be assimilated, that is, lose their cultural and ethnic identities.

13. *Do most Turks residing in America maintain their family and cultural ties to Turkey? In what ways, and more so or less so than other immigrants? If you have children born here, how do those children view their Turkish origins?*

Most Turks do maintain strong family and cultural ties to Turkey, probably more than other immigrants. These ties are quite strong to the extent that Turks in the U.S. do not integrate and participate in the American community and social activities. They tend to be closed in their own circles. For example, many Turks have Turkish TVs, follow the events in Turkey very closely. They are oblivious to what goes on in their own community in the U.S. Most of the time, children's ties are strong to Turkey. Even in the most "Wasp-ified" Turkish families in the U.S., the ties are there.

14. *What do think most Americans know of, or think about, Turkey? Are you satisfied with the level of the American public's understanding of your homeland? If not, what can or should be done to change or improve it?*

Americans do not know much about Turkey. Their perceptions are mostly based on stereotypes created by the American media and by the very negative activities of ethnic lobbies. Recently, with the increase of tourism between U.S. and Turkey and increased efforts of the Turkish American community and Turkish government in promoting a more balanced image of Turkey, there has been some improvement. Also the recent political situation [Editor's note: the war in Afghanistan] helped. Most important is the people-to-people connection [described in the second chapter of this book]. I am amazed that so much is going on between Turkey and the Melungeon community—which will eventually change the image of the Turks in the U.S.

15. *Any parting thoughts on the Melungeon-Turkish connection and what the future might bring, or what you personally would like to see as a development?*

I think the relationship can help both communities greatly in terms of public relations, joint cultural and social activities, combined power in legislative issues. As we move on to the "politically correct" climate in race relations and get away from the exclusive "Eurocentric" thinking, this relationship can only get better.

16. *Regarding the ATAA, what is your formal position within ATAA and how active are you in the organization? Why did you join? What is the purpose of ATAA and does it serve its purpose?*

I am the regional vice president of ATAA for Maryland, D.C., Virginia, and West Virginia. I have recently retired and I now can give a lot of time to ATAA activites. I joined ATAA mainly to activate the Turkish Americans in grassroots activities and sensitize them to the political process in the U.S. ATAA is a national umbrella organization with 55 local Turkish-American associations within its framework. ATAA's objective is to promote Turkish culture and heritage through the U.S. and also strive to organize the Turkish communities to be more active and vocal in their communities.

17. *What do you think needs to be emphasized and what should be de-emphasized?*

The emphasis must be in the positive and in the future. Too often, the Turkish community acts defensively because of the activities of the ethnic lobbies and also not doing their homework. For example we always react strongly to the so-called Armenian genocide resolution while it is out, but rarely contact our legislators at other times when it is dormant.

We need to emphasize the many good aspects of Turkey, its history, culture, tourism, secular Islam, the social and financial reforms, trade, business opportunities, strategic location and defense alliance, etc. What needs to be de-emphasized is the frantic reactions to ethnic lobby accusations. We can only prevent such reactions by being proactive with the media and the legislators. We need to create good and objective programs about issues which are frequently used to attack us and publicize them all the time. Another area of emphasis should be forming alliances with groups in the U.S. We already work closely with the Azerbaijani and Jewish groups—not as closely as we want yet. We need to develop new alliances. That is why the Melungeon and Native American connections would be so valuable.

18. *What do you see as the future of ATAA? How will it change? Should it change?*

I see growth and development in the future of ATAA. I was present twenty-two years ago when ATAA was formed and we have grown stronger every year. In terms of change, ATAA needs more professional staff and to have offices set up in key states in the U.S. Also, ATAA needs to put greater emphasis on grassroots activities, on educating the Turkish Americans how to be more active in their communities and in the legislative issues. This is one area where the Turks are quite inactive. I see this as the most important mission of ATAA.

19. *How will an enhanced understanding of the possible Native American and Melungeon connections to Turkic people enhance Turkish lobbying efforts in the U.S., if at all? How might it change the day-to-day lives of Turkish-Americans, Native Americans, and Melungeons? Will this be good, or bad, or of no relevance to mainstream America?*

I see great potential in the connections between Turks, Melungeons, and Native Americans in terms of lobbying efforts and voting capacity. The three groups need to know each other better and communicate more. Recently we met with Virginia Lieutenant Governor Tim Kaine—Brent could not attend. When I mentioned our connections to Melungeons, Mr. Kaine was very interested and took note. This connection needs to be publicized in an articulate and clear-cut manner—your book [this present text] will do a lot of that. The connection may not affect the day-to-day life of the individuals, but overall will bring great awareness to the Turks in terms of their ancient and recent history. I think this will be an excellent and unique example of the "ethnic connection-ethnic pot" phenomenon in the U.S. and, if properly publicized, it will definitely have relevance to mainstream America.

* | * | *

○ *Tolga Çubukçu*   Former president, Assembly of Turkish American Associations (ATAA). Interview completed by Brent Kennedy (e-mail/telephone) on 17 August 2000.

1. *Were you born in the U.S. or did you immigrate here? If the latter, why did you come?*

My family and I came to the U.S.A. in 1980. Our basic reason was the children's education.

2. *Why have you stayed?*

We liked it here, we found many friends and became a part of the community.

3. *Have you become a U.S. citizen? If so, why?*

Yes. To be able to vote, to be more active and integrate fully.

4. *What do you find positive in your experience as a Turkish American in the U.S.? Negative? Any discrimination toward you or your family?*

Being Turkish-American posed no hardship, and we faced no discrimination.

5. *What would you most like to change in the Turkish-American relationship? Why? How would you change it?*

The average American knows very little about Turks and Turkey, and what they know is not necessarily factual. In addition to the efforts of Turkish-Americans, the Turkish government also needs to play a very active role in disseminating information.

6. *When did you first hear that some Native American tribes might have Turkic roots?*

About five or six years ago.

7. *What did you think or feel about this possibility? Have you read/heard much about this? How strong/weak do you think the evidence is for such connections?*

Well, Turks have a long history and nomadic nature, and such a connection is possible.

8. *If true, how significant is this relationship (or how significant can it become) for Turks, Turkish-Americans, and Native Americans?*

I am hoping the relationship can be scientifically proven.

9. *When did you first hear that the Melungeons might have connections to Ottoman period Turks and other Ottoman subjects?*

Five or six years ago.

10. *What did you think or feel about this possibility? Have you read/heard much about this? How strong/weak do you think the evidence is for such connections?*

I've read and heard much about this. I've heard of positive evidence in favor of such a connection.

11. *If true, how significant is this relationship (or how significant can it become) for Turks, Turkish-Americans, and Melungeon-Americans?*

If true, it shall have an important role in strengthening the Turkish-American community in America. The number of voters is of great importance to being heard.

12. *What is the place of Turkish Americans? Should they emphasize their "Turkishness" or simply become absorbed into the so-called American "melting pot"?*

We should be Americans with Turkish roots. We need to protect and nurture Turkish culture and traditions, because Turks have an ancient history of culture, customs, traditions, and food and are, above all, a people with firm ties to their roots.

13. *Do most Turks residing in America maintain their family and cultural ties to Turkey? In what ways, and more so or less so than other immigrants? If you have children born here, how do they view their Turkish origins?*

After living in the U.S. for some time, Turks who were not born here tend to embrace the comforts, the orderliness, and the laws of the land, to the extent that they choose the civilization over their homesickness. The majority do not leave the U.S. throughout their working years. At the same time, however, and even if they lead comfortable lives, and achieve great wealth, they yearn for their country, for they cannot find in America the warmth, hospitality, and friendship they had enjoyed in Turkey. So they vacation there and many of the retirees also move back. Those born in the U.S. adapt to the system immediately, and foster sentiments different from their parents. It is a challenge to teach them Turkish and raise them in the Turkish culture. When these children reach 20-25 years of age, they start wondering about their roots and about half of them show an interest in visiting Turkey.

14. *What do you think most Americans know of, or think about, Turkey? Are you satisfied with the level of the American public's understanding of your homeland? If not, what can or should be done to change or improve it?*

Unfortunately, they know very little and what they do know is the product of widespread propaganda disseminated by the enemies of Turks, that is, the film *Midnight Express*, the allegations of human rights violations, etc. Despite this, any American who has actually visited Turkey and known some Turks becomes a friend and advocate of the people and the country. Finally, Americans know so little about Turkey that when they do find out, they are amazed at the misperceptions they may have heard.

15. *Any parting thoughts on the Melungeon-Turkish connection and what the future might bring, or what you personally would like to see as a development?*

An increase in the number of people defending Turkey's thesis, and an increase in the number of people who are her friends, may serve to diminish the negative propaganda and publications.

16. *Regarding ATAA, what is your formal position within ATAA and how active are you in the organization? Why did you join? What is the*

purpose of ATAA and does it serve its purpose? What do you think needs to be emphasized and what should be de-emphasized?

ATAA is a bridge between the peoples of the U.S. and Turkey. Our website describes our goals. We are working to improve the image of Turkey in this country. I have been actively working for the Turkish-American community for the past twenty years and, currently, I am the president of the ATAA. In addition to responding to unjust or biased allegations about Turkey, we are also working with other NGOs [NGO = nongovernmental organization] (both in Turkey and the U.S.) to promote and recognize Turkish culture, art, historic riches, and her vast tourism potential. You may know that this summer we took an ATAA delegation to Greece, in an attempt to contribute our share to the recent rapprochement.

17. *What do you see as the future of ATAA? How will it change? Should it change?*

We should reach more people. We need to find the resources to travel, hold lectures and seminars, take part in volunteering for the American community.

18. *How will an enhanced understanding of the possible Native American and Melungeon connections to Turkic people enhance Turkish lobbying efforts in the U.S., if at all? How might it change the day-to-day lives of Turkish-Americans, Native Americans, and Melungeons? Will this be good, or bad, or of no relevance to mainstream America?*

The greater the amount of Turkic people, the stronger the lobbying, to be sure.

* | * | *

○ *Osman Faruk Loğoğlu* Ambassador to the United States, Republic of Turkey, Turkish Embassy, Washington, D.C. Written interview: 26 April 2002.

1. *How did you first learn about the Melungeons and their possible connection to Turks and Ottoman populations?*

I had several conversations with Dr. Özdoğan who gave me some materials and one of your books. It goes without saying that my answers are my own personal views and do not in any way reflect the views of the Turkish Foreign Ministry.

I was named ambassador of Turkey to the U.S. in June 2001, arrived on 24 September and presented at the White House my Letter of Credence to President Bush on 10 October 2001. My prior diplomatic assignments include positions in the Foreign Ministry in Ankara, the last being the under secretary of the Foreign Ministry just before coming to Washington, D.C. My foreign assignments, starting from first to last: Turkish Mission to the European Union (Brussels, Belgium); Turkish Embassy (Dhakka, Bangladesh); Turkish Mission to the United Nations (New York); consul general (Hamburg, Germany); ambassador (Copenhagen, Denmark); ambassador (Baku, Azerbaijan).

2. *How have you been accepted thus far? Any discrimination?*

We have been accepted well in Washington, D.C. No problems. All we have seen has been positive.

3. *What would you most like to change in the Turkish-American relationship? Why? How would you change it?*

I would like to enhance trade and economic relations between Turkey and the U.S. While our relationship is strong in the political, defense, security, and related realms, our trade is not what it could be. There is also little American direct investment in Turkey. Moreover, there should be more Americans going to Turkey. The way to do it is to increase awareness in this country of the opportunities that exist in Turkey. This is why I am doing a lot of traveling in this country to bring Turkey to all corners of the U.S.A., not just the capital and New York city.

4. *When did you first hear that some Native American tribes might have Turkic/Central Asian roots?*

I first read about it in some Turkish newspapers some years ago.

5. *What did you think or feel about this possibility? Have you read/heard much about this? How strong/weak do you think the evidence is for such connections?*

I found the possibility not only interesting and touching, but also significant. From what I have seen and read so far, I think existing evidence warrants further research into the matter. Given the fact that Turks have always been mobile and on the move and the fact that they have moved in all directions by any means available to them, it would not be surprising that the Melungeons have Turkish ancestors. Research by scholars should be encouraged.

6. *If true, how significant is this relationship (or how significant can it become) for Turks, Turkish-Americans, and Native Americans?*

Such a connection would add a new dimension to the texture of our relations. It would create a strong bond between peoples who already feel friendship for one another.

7. *When did you first hear that the Melungeons might have connections to Ottoman-period Turks and other Ottoman subjects?*

Again, I read about it in Turkish newspapers some several years ago.

8. *What did you think or feel about this possibility? Have you read/heard much about this? How strong/weak do you think the evidence is for such connections?*

Like in my answer to question 5, I believe the evidence so far justifies further examination of the matter. In any case, the subject matter is heart-warming and has a positive, constructive spin.

9. *If true, how significant is this relationship (or how significant can it become) for Turks, Turkish-Americans, and Melungeon-Americans?*

Same as my answer to question 6. I think the Turkish people embrace the Melungeons and have already much affection for them.

10. *What is the place of Turkish-Americans? Should they emphasize their "Turkishness" or simply become absorbed into the so-called American "melting pot"?*

Turkish Americans are proud, productive American citizens. One thing about Turkish communities abroad is that they never give up their ties to the mother country. The call of the motherland is like an

ingrained lullaby in the minds of Turks everywhere. The strength of
the U.S.A. lies in the fact that the integrating identity of American
citizenship draws on the cultural diversity of the various groups that
make up this nation. In the melting-pot concept, the emphasis is more
on the "pot" than on "melting." Hence, it is only natural for the
Turkish Americans, like other groups in the U.S., to be Americans
first, while enriching their contribution to society through their
particular background.

11. *What do think most Americans know of, or think about, Turkey? Are
you satisfied with the level of the Amercican public's understanding of
your homeland? If not, what can or should be done to change or improve
it?*

Knowledge about Turkey among the Americans is rather limited.
The understanding of Turkey in the U.S. could and must be better.
Since the horrific events of September 11, appreciation of Turkey and
what it stands for has improved in this country. The one great asset
in this country is that not being informed about Turkey does not
automatically translate into being prejudiced against Turkey. So with
hard work, progress can be made. To this end, (a) the educational
system could be motivated to include more courses about foreign
lands, (b) Mass media could be more instrumental in educating the
public, (c) more contacts should be encouraged between scholars,
students and NGOs [nongovernmental organizations], (d) tourism
should be enhanced, [and] (e) the negative propaganda of known anti-
Turkish lobbies should be more effectively countered.

12. *Any parting thoughts on the Melungeon-Turkish connection and what
the future might bring, or what you personally would like to see as a
development?*

These connections would bring a new dimension and add human
interest to the relationship between Turkey and the U.S.A. I think that
it will definitely make a contribution to mainstream America. I say
to the Melungeons that we already embrace you and respect your
identity. As we get to know each other better, I believe this bond will
grow closer and stronger in the years to come.

* | * | *

o *Türker Özdoğan*   Professor and department head, Ceramics
Department, George Washington University,
Washington, D.C. Interview: 6 August 2002.

1. *Were you born in the U.S. or did you immigrate here? If the latter,
why did you come?*

I was sponsored by George Washington University as a faculty
member for my green card (my permanent resident visa). Once I
received my green card, I became a citizen through the normal
process.

2. *What do you find positive in your experience as a Turkish-American
in the U.S.? Negative? Any discrimination toward you or your family?*

Positive: I have found that the State Department and the Defense
Department have been most praising of Turks and due to their
influence in this country and in Washington, D.C., I have received
that support as well. However, the anti-Turkish lobby, particularly the
Greeks and Armenians, have tried to reduce this positive image.
However, I have felt protected from that lobby by the government
and related influential world experts who are very supportive of
Turkey.

Negative: Nothing. I have always found the experience to be
most positive. My family and I have never faced discrimination. As
a matter of fact, I have been praised for the positive image of Turks
in this country in regard to the Korean War and its close
governmental ties with Turkey.

3. *What would you most like to change in the Turkish-American
relationship? Why? How would you change it?*

I would like to see more cultural exchange to promote Turkish
culture in the U.S. and U.S. culture in Turkey. This should include
a better understanding of the historical and anthropological ties of
both nations which date back to ancient times with the migration of
Native Americans to North America.

4. *When did you first hear that some Native American tribes might have
Turkic (Central Asian) roots?*

I was seventeen years old (circa 1960) when I first discovered these ties as part of my interest in the similarities between Turkish flat-woven tapestries called "kilims" and Native American blankets.

5. What did you think or feel about this possibility? Have you read/heard much about this? How strong/weak do you think the evidence is for such connections?

After arriving in the U.S., my interest became very high and during my personal research in this subject I found the evidence for this connection becoming quite strong. In particular, I found significant religious, artistic, linguistic, and genetic similarities. Many anthropologists have found a continuous flow of culture from Turkic peoples into North America.

6. If true, how significant is this relationship (or how significant can it become) for Turks, Turkish-Americans, and Native Americans?

Since we have found that the genetic and linguistic evidence is so clear, the cultural similarities are strongly supported and hence this relationship is quite significant.

7. When did you first hear that the Melungeons might have connections to Ottoman period Turks and other Ottoman subjects?

About ten years ago I became familiar with the Melungeon connection through the Melungeon Heritage Society's activities, especially Dr. Brent Kennedy's work on the subject.

8. What did you think or feel about this possibility? Have you read/heard much about this? How strong/weak do you think the evidence is for such connections?

I was very excited about the possibility of a Melungeon connection and feel it is quite likely due to linguistic and historic evidence. This connection is extremely exciting for both Turks and Americans. The citizens of both nations have an unusually strong interest in this issue because it should further encourage the great kinship between them.

9. *If true, how significant is this relationship (or how significant can it become) for Turks, Turkish-Americans, and Melungeon-Americans?*

This kinship between Turks and Melungeons and Native Americans will clearly enhance the image of the Turkic people in the U.S. This will be seen as a discovery of a very fundamental connection between the U.S. and the Turkish world of over 200 million people. This means a stronger connection with the Turkish states of the former Soviet Union. It is also a connection between cultures that occupy some of the largest land areas in the world. It is like finding a diamond in the rough. It is a blessing for Turks and Americans and, I believe, the entire world.

10. *What is the place of Turkish-Americans? Should they emphasize their "Turkishness" or simply become absorbed into the so-called American "melting pot"?*

Turks should be absorbed into the "melting pot" while not forgetting their Turkish heritage. The addition of Turkish culture will only make the "melting pot" richer.

11. *Do most Turks residing in America maintain their family and cultural ties to Turkey? In what ways, and more so or less so than other immigrants? If you have children born here, how do those children view their Turkish origins?*

Yes, they definitely maintain their cultural and familial ties to Turkey. It is probably stronger than other immigrants because Turks are somewhat less well known than other Western immigrants and there are not a great number of Turks in the U.S. The children look upon their Turkish roots with pride and great interest.

12. *What do you think most Americans know of, or think about, Turkey? Are you satisfied with the level of the American public's understanding of your homeland? If not, what can or should be done to change or improve it?*

The knowledge of Turkey by the general public, outside of many governmental officials, is low or misinformed. The Assembly of Turkish American Associations (ATAA), including the Melungeon

Heritage Association, must work very hard to inform the public of the reality of the Turkic world, and especially Atatürk's Turkey.

13. *Any parting thoughts on the Melungeon-Turkish connection and what the future might bring, or what you personally would like to see as a development?*

The connected Turkic peoples of Asia Minor and Central Asia who came to North America through the Bering Strait and across the Atlantic Ocean, respectively, are reconnected in North America through the intermarriage of Native Americans and Melungeons. This is an incredible and beautiful concept. I also feel that Turkic peoples of the world are extremely blessed to have this connection with Native Americans. In fact, it is a double blessing to have Native Americans, Anatolian Turks, and Central Asian Turks united in this blessed land. One can even say that this ancestral relationship is a model for the ideal world citizenship.

* | * | *

o   *Nur Serter*   Vice rector and faculty member, professor of Economics, Istanbul University. Interview: in Prof. Serter's office, 25 July 2000. (Interviewed in English by Kennedy and Scolnick, with Sami Ferliel present to translate as needed.)

1. *When did you first hear of the Melungeons and the Melungeon story and what was your first impression?*

I first heard of this when you [Kennedy] came to a visit with the rector of Istanbul University. When I heard the Melungeon story from you, I then remembered that I had heard the story in the newspapers as well. So I can say I heard the story directly from Brent Kennedy.

2. *What do you think about the story today, now having been to the United States and having visited with the Melungeons, having read additional information, and having seen the latest evidence? What's your impression of the story now?*

I think there are two aspects. The first one is you are making a scientific research, so what solutions you get in this research are very important. As far as I know, as far as I have read, I think the scientific results are clear, and the Melungeon story is not just a story anymore. It is a reality and that is important. And the second aspect, it's a humanitarian aspect maybe. I think it's important for humanity to make a contact between nations. I believe that today most of the Melungeons have sympathy for Turkey. And Turkish people have great sympathy and love and respect for the Melungeon community, and for those Americans, too, connected to the Melungeons. I think that this second aspect is very, very important.

3. *What further work needs to be done, if any, especially relating to the additional evidence? Is there additional work to be done?*

I think that the research is continuing—it's going on. And as far as I know the evidence that has appeared today shows a relationship between Turks and Melungeons. But I think the research has to continue and we have to reach more concrete evidence. But in another way, I want to say that for me it's not important to find more concrete evidence. If people feel they have a bond with Turkish people and with Turkey, I think that's very important for me. I feel that Melungeons are feeling that way and we are feeling that way.

4. *You mentioned earlier the great affection the Turkish people have for the Melungeons. There is so much media coverage here as well. Even in the more remote villages the people know about, and are excited about, the Melungeons. What is it that goes to the hearts and minds of the Turkish people that makes the story so intriguing and romantic for them?*

The United States is a dream for most Turkish people. And to see something there that is from their blood, something from their ancestors that has contributed to the American nation is important to them. It excites them and it is an honor to be represented in the United States. That's important. And I think when you see you and people who are representative of the Melungeon story, they like you. The Turkish people are a people full of love, so they get excited. They like you, they love you, they want to get in contact with you. But there's a second side to this story. You represent personally, N. Brent Kennedy, as well, and I think that is very important. You have important things to say that people want to hear.

5. What effects, if any, do you see the Melungeon and Turkish connection having on Turkish-American foreign policy and Turkish-American relations?

Well, I think it depends on what is being done in the United States. When there are lobbies in the United States . . . I don't think we've ever had a strong lobby in the United States. And I think this is going to make a great contribution for a Turkish lobby—to make Turkey understandable. I want the foreign ministers of the United States and also the people in the government to understand Turkey, to learn something about Turkey, and to get acquainted with the Turkish people. If they do understand Turkish people, they will feel a great sympathy for Turkey and her people. Through this way, through the Melungeon story, they will get more acquainted with Turkey, Turkish people, and they will understand Turkey better. Personal relationships are important, so by this way it will contribute to the foreign policy of the United States. But I think it will take a long time. I don't expect anything in the short term.

6. The Melungeon story has drawn the interest of Turks from all sides, the left, the right, the center. Do you think that the interest that comes from, say, Islamists, or the so-called Gray Wolves [ultranationalists], or even moderates stems from a true, across-the-board interest in the Melungeon story, or could it be simply a self-serving interest that varies from party to party and interest group to interest group?

Well, I can't answer this accurately because I think for some it is a true interest, but there may be some groups who would like to use this for their own interest.

7. Should the Turkish government be more involved in the Melungeon story, or should it continue as it has been—people to people, educational institution to educational institution, and town to town?

No, I do not think the government should be more involved in this issue. I'm afraid that if government is involved, then it could turn out to be a political movement. I don't like Melungeons to be involved in politics, especially Turkish inner politics.

In reference to your previous question, there are many different groups in Turkey and some of these groups would like to make contact with you to say that your blood, your culture, and so forth comes from middle Asia and you are Turks ethnically, and nothing else. I don't believe there is a pure race in the world. All the races are mixed with one another. There is a political movement like this in Turkey. So I'm afraid if politics are involved and politicians are involved, they'll try to take the Melungeon people and carry them into their inner policies.

8. *You mentioned earlier that the Turkish people admire the United States and see us as a great nation, and the Melungeons as their connection to it. How does the Turkish-Melungeon-American relationship influence the way the Turkish people—and that could be a governmental leader, an educator, or a fisherman in the Aegean region—how does this developing relationship influence the way average Turkish people feel about the world and their place in it?*

I think some of us will say that our ancestors have gone elsewhere and made a contribution there. And some will feel that it is wonderful that you are making contact with us, that you are not running away from being partly Turkish. On the contrary, you are trying to find some evidence and make connections with your Turkish ancestors. That will be important for them (the Turkish people) to know that we are not just a people alone in one place in the world.

9. *What would your hopes be for the Turkish and American people over the next decade?*

I think [their relationship] will improve. People are going from one country to another much more so. Our young people are now learning more about each other. If the governments are not involved, I think people of the two countries will solve all their other problems. I don't think we have any serious problems with the United States. Beyond politics, average human beings can solve their problems if they have contact.

10. *Is there anything else that you can think of? Any thoughts that you may have regarding the Turkish-Melungeon relationship? Any aspirations or dreams or hopes that you may have about where all this is going?*

First of all, I really felt very good when I met you. I felt that you were sincere, because you showed us that people from other continents and other nations could get together and share love, sympathy, thoughts, and peace. I think there is a message that all humanity must take from this Melungeon story—it is peace for the world, peace for humanity. We don't know from which country or which continent our great-great grandparents came. And I don't believe there is anyone in the world that can say I am a pure race, I represent a pure race, or that I come from a specific place in the world. It is not possible. Everyone in the world has mixed up. So I think one message is peace, but another is also that everyone should think, "I have ancestors from other nations, other parts of the world, so I should leave behind all the bad thoughts. I shouldn't think bad things of them. I shouldn't think of any nation as my enemy. We can be sisters, brothers. I may have grandparents living in those countries or nations. . . . " I think what the world should get from this Melungeon story is peace.

* | * | *

○ *Hayri Ulgen*   Dean, faculty of Business and Economics, Istanbul University. Interview: 25 July 2000 in Dean Ulgen's office. Interviewed in English and Turkish by Kennedy and Scolnick, with Sami Ferliel present to assist in translation.

1. *When did you first hear of the Melungeon story and what was your impression?*

I was really astonished when I first heard about the Melungeons. At first I didn't believe it, but then you spoke to our faculty two years ago. When I heard your conference it was clear that the names and words were connected. These were real Turkish words. I believe central Asian people went to America by the Bering Strait, so I thought, well maybe they also came this way [post-Columbus] as well. When you presented your theory that these people were the descendants of Levants and maybe captured by the Spanish or Portuguese, and were perhaps sold with Black people to America, it is really possible. Why not? It happened in other places at that time. Of course, we need to research customs . . . and other areas as well.

2. *What sort of evidence do we need to absolutely convince people? What sort of evidence would be most convincing to you as a scholar and an academic?*

Well, the genetics is most convincing, which I believe you already have. [Laughs.] But I recently read in *Sabah* a story about Melungeons and the writer said that the Melungeons must be Turks because they say that they are Turks! According to Atatürk, that is all that is needed to be a Turk.

3. *To what extent are the people in Turkey interested in Melungeons? Is the Melungeon story something of interest to the average person in Turkey?*

You know, we have some customs in Turkey. We want to help people. When there are problems in Chechnia, Kavkazia, or Azerbaijan, we normally want to help them. This is a Turkish custom. For example, if we see people like the Melungeons in America, we say, "Oh, people of our blood. We want to help them!" But in this case, you don't need our help. You are not asking anything of us. Normally people want something from our side. So this is a good occasion for us, because we have found a group that says they are from Turkey, but they don't need something from us. I have another brother in the United States now. He is Turkish and he is American, and Americans are partly Turkish. Why not? You know, we have some problems in expressing ourselves to other countries. You know, a normal American would never think what you think . . . they don't know. To a normal American if you ask, Where is Turkey?, Where is Istanbul?, maybe they know Istanbul—where it is—but Ankara they don't know. To a normal American if a man says "I am from Turkey," they don't know Turkey. But in our case, we read about the Mississippi, New Orleans, San Francisco, and the history of the United States. We study this in our schools. But you don't study this—you specialize (only in your own country). So, in our case I think Turks will be very interested in the Melungeon [connection]. They believe that Melungeons are Turks and like us, warmhearted, and in the United States.

4. *Which groups within Turkey—business, governmental, political, or academic—will have an interest in the Melungeons?*

Political people will be very interested. Industrial [business] people, too, will be interested, of course. Everything is economic now. But from the political side they must be very interested. Next is academics, Turkish Studies departments, for example. Medical issues, languages, folk traditions are also important. You know, people want to find their ancestry. You want to know from where you come. This is the nature of human beings. With Melungeons, there is so much to study [and] interest will be in many, many areas.

5. *Will the cultural exchanges, the visits, the developing relations have any effect on Turkish foreign policy, or American foreign policy toward Turkey?*

Yes, it can influence. Really, it can. For example, our students who are sent to your university [the University of Virginia's College at Wise], they increase each year—two, four, six, then eight, maybe someday twenty. Our students lived with the Melungeon families and they came home and said to their families, "The Melungeons do this, and the Melungeons do that, and that the Melungeons are Turkish [in their customs and their habits]." Day to day there is support from the Melungeons. We know they [the Melungeons] don't need our money or our help—all they want is to find out if they are Turkish. *Kardesler* [brothers]. This cannot help but influence foreign policy at some point.

6. *Should the Turkish government in any way be involved in this story, or should the government stay totally out of it?*

No, but the government should also be concerned about this business. When we try to go for an answer from the Common Market, for example, we have many people in Germany, and in the Dutch parliament, and in France. If we had some Melungeons in the United States, well . . . not bad. This is a real lobby, you know. In ten years, or maybe five years, we may all be studying English. We may have different customs, but we will maybe be one world. We are coming from Asia, all of us, and if we can prove that, it will bring people together—whatever their country or color.

7. *How does all this information, these new ideas and the education of the people in both the United States and Turkey about their probable kinship, influence the way in which Turks view themselves and their place and role in the world? Will learning that there are people in the United States of Turkish or Ottoman ancestry make modern Turks feel less alone in the world?*

In the global world, I don't think that we are surrounded by enemies anymore. Because everything has changed. I have so many Greek friends, for example. The governments have some problems. They also don't believe we are enemies, but they do it for show, in my opinion. When I go to Greece, we love each other, we conduct business and we always speak about the past tense. We have good relations with Romania, with Bulgaria, Armenia, too. And we want to open the gates to Armenia. If we market something to Armenia, they will economically grow. Maybe they will come from Azerbaijan, also, because it's all economics. Most problems can be solved by economics. If they have money, if they have different positions, they change. People change. Let us talk a bit about Turkish people. There are Turkish people from Central Asia, Turkish people from Istanbul, from Anatolia, Asia Minor, and from Europe. And from the United States. They don't say that they are Turks. They don't want to say that they are Turks. There are so many who are successful, who earn a lot of money, in the stock market for example, in factories, in the entertainment business. But, sadly, they don't want to say they are Turks. But if the Turkish economy is higher and looks like it does in Japan or France, they would say, "I am Turkish-American." The Melungeons are pioneers, really. They said, "We are Turks." No one forced them to say this and they are not ashamed. You may be [a] small community, but you are leading the way. Perhaps other families will see this and be proud and do the same. In Turkmenistan and other Turkish countries, they are now saying, "We are Turks." Turks are becoming one of the biggest populations. Turks can be Muslims, or Christians, or Buddhists, or Jews. It doesn't matter. But one must first not feel ashamed of who he is. I think this is what Melungeons are teaching.

8. *What else would you like to say about the Melungeon story, or the relationship between Turks and Melungeons, or what your hopes for the future might be?*

In the future, the Turks of the world must come to feel themselves to be a worldwide community, a global community like the Chinese, or Japanese, feel themselves to be. Some countries see themselves as existing only within their boundaries, but we are in almost all countries, not just Turkey. There are Turks in northern India, northern Iran and Iraq. Israel. If we understand this, then it makes it more difficult to hate other nations. This is true for all people, I think, but they need people like the Melungeons to show them this fact.

||*

o *Turan Yazgan* President, Turkish World Research Foundation, Istanbul, Turkey. Interview: 20 April 2001. Translated by Prof. Sami Ferliel.

1. *How long have you been interested in the study of Turkish peoples?*

Not the desire for studying Turkish peoples, but the desire for reaching them has been with me since my first grade in high school. I even recall vowing on the back of a photograph with a friend of mine, who also appears in the photograph taken in those days, that one day we would go to the region of Turkistan, which we had marked on a map. This photo and its reverse side I still have.

2. *How did this interest arise in you?*

There is no doubt that my primary school teacher had a great role in the arousal of this passion. But I believe that this interest is truly a dictate of God. Because my father, who was an illiterate person, named my elder brothers with Arabic names, he called me Turan [translator's note: the name associated with a pan-Turkish state]. I believe this to be a divine coincidence. Besides, I also actualized another dream of my high school boyhood by giving my own sons the names of the Turkish Kaan [Grand Turkish Emperor], also a blessing of God. My son's names are Karahan, Korhan, and Kozhan. Further, in my later life, I had the honor of stepping for the first time into every corner of the Turkish World, having with me groups of 160 people. This has truly been a blessing of God on me.

3. *What captured and held your interest?*

The previous answer, I think, can also be taken as a reply to this question.

4. *What kind of outcome do you expect from current and future research?*

New studies regarding the Turkish world have greatly changed our historical knowledge and will continue to do so. If we want to summarize these changes, we can make the following remarks.

The Turks are absolutely *not* a nomadic nation. They have, within the framework of the history of world civilization, created a special civilization of technological discoveries and inventions of great importance to the civilized world (ironwork, various wheels, horsemanship, implementation of animal industry for human nourishment, and such life-changing elements as paper, gun powder, and a printing press).

They have carried out excavations in Pazirik Kurgan, Işik Göl, and Birka that have confirmed the continuing evolvement and improvement of Turkish culture since B.C. times.

We believe that the present excavations being carried out in Bayram Kurgan, which is located on the peak of the Altai Mountains overlooking Mongolia, will contribute greatly significant information to our present knowledge.

DNA testing, and particularly Y chromosome testing, have proved the kinship between the builders of America's glorious Native American civilizations and the Turks in Yakutistan. We believe that we still need a lot more studies on similarities between America's declined civilization and Asia's civilization.

5. *Please tell us about the Turkish World Research Foundation. What are its activities? What kind of organization does it have? How is it financed? Is it connected in any way with the Turkish Government? How do you see the future of the Foundation and what is the significance of its work? And what kind of significance will it bear in the future?*

The Foundation for Studies in the Turkish World was established on 20 July 1980. The initial step towards the Foundation was the Kutyay Center for Research and Publications, which I founded in 1972. The objective of the Foundation is, without imposing any limitation of time and place, to study Turks and carry out research on every aspect of their history and culture. In addition to this goal, it also aims to form relationships with Turks across the World so as to create cooperation in matters of language and ideas. In order to achieve this, the Foundation carries out educational, cultural, and social activities.

Our Foundation has a board of trustees comprising four members. The president of the board and the administrator, who has full authority in all activities, is me, Turan Yazgan. I have held this authority since the Foundation was established. In the headquarters of the Foundation there is a general director and two employees who coordinate domestic and international affairs respectively.

It is possible to divide the Foundation's activities into two areas: activities that provide financial resources and services.

Our main establishments that provide finances are two large Turkish restaurants (Daruzziyafe and Sehzade), the Telekom Payment Branch Office, the Aycell Cell Phone Company, the Kutbil Computer Management and Editing/Printing Facilities, and the Kutyay Education and Research Center. There are also some managements of which we are partners.

We can group our services under the following headings.

I. Publication Services
   Printed materials
   •*Türk Dunyası Tarih ve Kültür Dergisi* (*The Turkish World History and Culture Periodical*) printed monthly in color, 64 pages.
   •*Türk Dunyası Arastirmaları* (*Research in the Turkish World*) printed bimonthly, 240 pages.
   •*Bilgi ve Toplum Dergisi* (*Knowledge and Society Periodical*) printed as files are complete.
   •*Klasik Tûrk Muziği Nota Yayınları* (*Classical Turkish Music Notes*).

Films
•Documentaries: *Resulzâde* and *Gaspirali Ismail*.

Audio
•Records: set of classical Turkish music (six- and four-recording sets).
•Cassettes: same as records, with additional Turkish world music (two-cassette set).
•Computer discs: same as above.

II. Conferences
    •Scholarly meetings (at least twice per year at home and abroad).
    •Conferences
        Conference of the Assembly of Turkish Peoples.
        Women's Conferences of the Turkish World.
    •Festivals
        Turkish World Children's Festival (annually).
        Turkish World Circumcision (entry into adulthood) Festivals (various countries).
    •Lectures
        Weekly, in our Suleymaniye Cultural Center.
    •Concerts of Turkish World Music
        Our Turkish World Music Chorus has fifty-five members and has given concerts at home and abroad. Our two CDs comprising performances by this chorus are very popular both at home and abroad.

III. Educational Activities
    •Domestic
    –Courses in Turkish of Turkey for teachers who come from other Turkic nations.
    –Courses in Market Economy for bureaucrats who come from the Turkish World.
    –Courses in Banking and Insurance for the Turkish World bureaucrats.
    •Abroad
    A. Turkish World Cultural Centers.

The Turkish World Cultural Centers, which function as institutions of diffused education, also establish ties between local peoples, especially authors, scholars, scientists, publishers, and Turkey. They offer courses in Turkish on Turkey and Turkish affairs, aimed at the above people. They implement social and cultural activities under the direction of the centers' director. Activities relating to various aspects of our culture, such as Ramadan Breaking-fast dinners, holiday dinners, commemoration ceremonies held for great individuals of the Turkish World, art exhibitions and display of handiworks, studies in Turkish folklore, teaching the playing of Turkish musical instruments such as the Saz, and celebrations of the coming of spring are just a few examples. In addition, the centers organize relations between the Foundation and the country in question. For instance, those who will be entertained as guests of the Foundation are first required to apply to the Center. The Center determines the groups that will participate in the Turkish World Children's Festival, which is organized annually, and conducts the formalities. They supervise teachers, do joint work with them, and evaluate their extra curricular activities. They organize nationwide competitions in related countries and reward the winners. They form student groups from among those who are successful in their schools and reward them by giving them a chance to spend their holidays in Turkey as guests of the Foundation.

Finally, in places where there are no Turkish World cultural centers, school masters, deans, or department heads are required to function within their structures by performing any activity that is possible in a center and are entitled to use their money like center directors. Independent Turkish World Cultural centers are shown in the attached chart. In locations where there are no independent centers, the Foundation's high schools and Turkish language departments can function as centers.

■ **Turkish World Cultural Centers** ■

Cuvasistan	Cubuksari Turkish World Cultural Center	Kuksumskaya Ave. 11 PTU N.18, Cubuksari
Tataristan	Tataristan Calli Turkish World Cultural Center	Suyumbike Ave. Komp. 51/02-B

Tataristan	Tataristan Kazan Turkish World Cultural Center Cultural Center	Gaskar Kamal Ave. 80. Mektep Kazan—Tataristan
Macedonia	Gostivar Turkish World Matukar	12. Noyamvri Ave. 37/A Gostivar—Macedonia
Kosovo	Kosovo Turkish World Cultural Center	Kosova Prizren Kasaboc Association of Turkish Prizren—Kosova
Gagauzyeri	Gagauzyeri Turkish World Cultural Center	Lenin Street 204 A Komrat Gagauzeri—Moldova
Bulgaria	Bulgaria Kircali Turkish World Cultural Center	Kircali PK 241 Blvd. Bulgaria No. 41 Kircali—Bulgaria
Hakasya	Hakas Turkish World Culture Center	Icetinkina Ave. N. 23 Abakan—Hakasya

B. Turkish World High Schools

The Foundation for Studies in the Turkish World applies two methods in running its high schools. According to the first method—as is the case with the Turkish World Baku Atatürk High School—excluding the building, the high school belongs completely to the Foundation. The only administrator is the director who comes to his post by appointment. Excluding the teachers sent from Turkey, to choose local teachers and appoint them, to conduct all legal and other formalities, which are necessary for running the school, is entirely the director's responsibility. This is quite an expensive way to operate a high school, but it provides the Foundation with complete control.

According to the second method, an existing local high school is chosen with which an agreement is signed. A director is appointed from Turkey, and this director is held responsible for running Turkish courses. The director, with a sufficient number of teachers, starts teaching Turkish at the sixth or ninth grades. If it is a high school with eleven grades, teaching Turkish begins at the first grade. The director has no say in courses other than Turkish. Courses in general Turkish History, Religion, and Morality are also offered by the

Foundation's teachers. If a high school makes a request for teachers of other courses, then the Foundation tries to provide them through its own means. This second method is less expensive and is sufficient in meeting the Foundation's purpose. Such high schools are willing to achieve the status of the Baku Atatürk High School, if the Foundation's resources can meet their expenses. In this case, local teachers would get their salaries directly from the Foundation and they would achieve a higher standard of living than normally available to them. The Foundation's high schools are listed in the chart below.

■ Turkish World High Schools ■

NAME	COUNTRY	TEACHERS	STUDENTS
Turkish World Atatürk High School	Azerbaycan	Turkey 7 Local 24	376
Turkish World Kentav Atatürk High School	Kazakistan	Turkey 3 Local 10	250
Turkish World Kazak Turkish High School (Kizilorda)	Kazakistan	Turkey 3 Local 10	285
Turkish World Calli Turkish—Tatar High School (No. 80, Calli)	Tataristan	Turkey 5 Local 10	295
Turkish World Calli Turkish—Tatar High School (No. 21, Calli)	Tataristan		
Turkish World Kazan Turkish-Tatar High School	Tataristan	Turkey 3 Local 27	180
Undesignated	Tataristan	Turkey 3	250

C. Higher Education.

The Foundation has three types of higher education.

1. In Cubuksari, Cuvasistan, the College for Interpretership and Computer Literacy.

High school graduates, following the completion of proficiency courses in Turkish, which are taught in the first year, continue their education in the second year with courses in computer literacy and

interpretership training. The goal of this college is to train inter-
mediary workers who can do translation work between Cuvasistan,
which is a Christian country, and Turkey, and also secretarial
services. In establishing and retaining relations in the fields of
tourism, trade, and industry, our graduates from this college have
been playing an important role. The college was established with the
structure of a vocational high school and now functions under the
auspices of the Cuvasistan State University.

■ The Turkish World Vocational College ■

NAME STUDENTS	COUNTRY	FACULTY
The Turkish World Cubuksari Vocational College	Cuvasistan	from Turkey 2 250

---

2. Turkish Language and Literature Departments
   The Foundation for Studies in the Turkish World has no university in any country. However, it has managed to get some universities
to open Turkish language departments within their structures and has
assumed all responsibility to operate these departments. Some of
these departments have been accredited by Turkey's Council for
Higher Education. Student placement in these departments is conducted by the Student Selection and Placement Center of Turkey and
the diplomas awarded are considered equal to those obtained in
Turkey. In this manner, the Foundation achieves its objective of training teachers of the Turkish of Turkey in the most cost-effective
manner.

■ Turkish World Turkish Language and Literature Departments ■

UNIVERSITY STUDENTS	COUNTRY	FACULTY
Korkut Ara University Turkish Language Department (Kizilorda)	Kazakistan	Turkey 3 250 Local 10

Abay University Turkish Language and Literature Department (Almati)	Kazakistan	Turkey 3 Local 10	285
Kazan Humaniter University Turkish Language Department	Tataristan	Turkey 5 Local 10	295
Kazan Education Institute Turkish Language Department	Tataristan	Turkey 3 Local 27	180
Turkish World Mohackale Dagistan Turkish Language Department	Dagistan	Turkey 2	50
Celalabad State University Turkish Language Department	Kirgizistan	Turkey 3	150

3. Colleges

The Foundation first opened an Institute of Business Management in the structure of Azerbaycan People's Savings Management Institute, and later on transformed it into the College of Business Management. A similar college was also established in the city of Celalabad, Kirgizistan. This college was founded within the structure of the Commerce Institute. Following the exertion of excessive pressure, it was transformed into a college of two departments: the Department of Business Management and the Department of Foreign Relations.

In the first college, in Baku, the form of administration was such: although the dean was from Turkey and all local faculty members received their salaries from the Foundation, all authority and control of the Institute and College were in the office of the Institute's president. Upon abolition of this Institute our college was consolidated into the Azerbaycan State University of Economics. At present, negotiations are in progress between this university and the Foundation for a new type of administration, and efforts continue to transform it into a comprehensive college of Turkey.

Our college in Kirgizistan is entirely under the control of the Foundation, as is the Turkish World Baku Atatürk High School. Excluding those faculty members sent from Turkey, the selection of local faculty and their appointment, as well as the responsibility for all legal and educational requirements, are under the authority of the dean, who is appointed by the Foundation.

Both colleges are accredited by Turkey's Council of Higher Education and diplomas are recognized as equal to those obtained in Turkey. Each year fifteen students in Celalbad and thirty students in Baku are selected and placed by the Student Selection and Placement Center.

Our Foundation provides its finances through its own and partner managements, the major ones of which were listed earlier. Additional sources of revenue that help with educational objectives include the Farabi Book-Selling Center, Ucok Wholesale Food Provision Company (100% owned by the Foundation), Ltd. (30% owned by the Foundation), unsolicited private donations, and some minimal support from the state (in 2002, this amounted to seven billion Turkish Lira, or about $7,000 U.S. dollars). We also receive a small allocation from the state's Promotion Fund for some of our programs, generally meeting no more than half of the cost of any specific programs. (As an example, we have received limited funding for three of our seven Children's Festivals.)

The Foundation has no ties with the government. It is a completely independent administrative, political, and financial entity. It functions as a free spirit in all that it undertakes. It unconditionally abides by the laws of Turkey and elsewhere where it functions. We strive to avoid daily politics in all of our efforts. It operates for the Turkish World with a policy of 25, 50, even 100 years ahead. With these characteristics, just like yesterday and today, it will always hold its ground. It does not need the state, businessmen, or the wealthy. It never yields. Undoubtedly it sets a unique example for Turkey. It is a fact that, officially and unofficially, at home and abroad, its work is praised by everybody. Both the Foundation and its president, who has been in office since the day it was founded, have been awarded more than 250 plaques and eighteen honorary doctorates. This speaks not to the importance of the person but to the value placed on our mission.

6. *When did you first hear about the Melungeons? What was your impression? What kind of results do you expect from ongoing research?*

I learned about the Melungeons from the Mayor of Çeşme, Nuri Ertan. And I felt a great interest, of course. However, I previously knew that the Ottoman sailors (the Levants) had been taken in significant numbers to America as captives. I also knew from previous study that Murat Reis (Captain Murat) had gone there with two ships, but had not returned and instead remained there. It made me happy to come face to face with those I feel could well be descended from some of the men. I believe that research needs to continue and I suspect that it will prove that the Melungeons are indeed Ottoman peoples, including Turks, who intermarried with Native Americans and others over the centuries. Of course, over time the Melungeons emerged as a separate ethnic group with its own identity and culture, which is what always happens. We do know that the Levants were generally heavily Turkish in their ethnic origin, as this was a requirement of that time period. We observe as well a strict selection process of the *seyhulislam* (the supreme religious authority who comes after Sadrazam, the prime iminster) in Ottoman history. In other words, I would expect a high degree of true Turkish culture and genes among the earliest Melungeon ancestors.

7. *What do you think about the evidence that has been discovered so far? What should be the aim of future research and study?*

It would be useful to continue Y chromosome tests, even mitochondrial DNA testing. From the Levants we should see the remnants of Central Asian and Mongolian-Siberian male lines, and possibly Middle Eastern, Balkans, and south Asian as well. With the Turkish families who also came to America as servants and settlers we should see evidence of the women through the mitochondria. It must also be noted that no significant work has been performed in the Ottoman archives. We hope that what is needed in the area would be provided by our Foundation if sufficient resources could be obtained.

8. *What is the significance of the Melungeon story?*

The Melungeon story is, above all, a matter of discovering the truth and holding on to this truth. And in this respect, it is a story of and dictate of humanity and dignity. It can be a model for other people who seek their own self-respect. The duty of scholars and scientists is to discover truths and display them, not dismiss them or cover them for purely political or self-serving reasons. Therefore, the Melungeon matter is not only a social and ethnic one but it is also a scientific one.

9. *What kind of place do the Melungeons have within the framework of studies conducted by the Foundation? When did you first hear that some Native Americans might also have an Ottoman or Central Asian connection? In your opinion, how sound is the evidence regarding this connection?*

As we have always remarked, we in the Foundation have the goal of studying Turkishness without imposing any limitations of time or place. Since the knowledge obtained so far gives us clues that the Melungeons have a Turkish connection, we need to take a special interest in this topic. For the time being, this interest of ours, which is rather platonic, is focused on creating ties of friendship. We proclaim to the entire world with great pride that we, the Foundation, feel much greater interest in Melungeons than they might feel in us.

To the second and third questions, it might be possible to find the most reliable evidence in tests which would show that Ottoman Levants mixed with Native Americans. When I first looked at Brent Kennedy's face, I was looking at my nephew. Physically, he is the twin brother of my nephew, Atakan Yazgan. While this is not DNA, physical phenotypes do tell us certain things about probable kinship. More significant than this, though, is that we felt immediate, brotherly affinity towards the Melungeons and they felt the same toward us. We connected on a cultural level, which was not surprising if we do indeed share common roots. While scientific studies continue, it is, in our view, a duty assigned to us by humanity to increase this heartfelt affinity. In order to fulfill this duty, we will continue to do our best, both in the direction of new studies and the direction of activities fostering friendship.

10. *Do Native American tribes in general interest the Foundation? In what ways? What kind of significance does this study bear for the Foundation?*

From our perspective, Native Americans have three attractive aspects. The first aspect is that long ago, when America and Asia were connected, it is likely that Turkic people who lived in Yakutistan and eastern Siberia emigrated to America. And let me add, it is also possible that those living in America crossed the other way and became some of our ancestors. DNA tests carried out on this subject have yielded some striking results. Besides, when Frank Keel (eastern director of the Bureau of Indian Affairs and a Choctaw-Chickasaw) participated in our conferences, he looked like a brother to the Yakutistan represenative, Mr. Okan, who is a Saka Turk. This struck everyone at the Conference and there was much talk about it.

Secondly, the position of the Uygur Turks, who escaped from Genghis Khan to America by way of the Sea of Japan is noteworthy. These people, who belonged to the Atabaskan language group, bear traces of the Turkish language and Turkish identity. Publications produced on this topic are quite satisfactory and our Foundation published one of them in translation (Ethel G. Stewart, *Dene-Na Dene Indian Migration: Turks Who Escaped from Genghiz Khan*, Publications of the Foundation for Studies in the Turkish World, Istanbul, 2000).

Third, we are interested in Native Americans because of Melungeons who emerged as a mixture of Levants and Native Americans, as well as other peoples. In addition to these points, we need to say that we are interested in them as a human drama. Native Americans, whose population might have reached a number of 500 million for both continents, have unfortunately been leveled by massacre and disease to a number which is suitable for museum study.

11. *What is the extent of knowledge of the Turkish people regarding the Melungeons' and some Native American tribes' possible connections to Turks?*

Unfortunately, the people of Turkey have very little knowledge about this subject in general. And the scanty knowledge that is available has reached a very small audience. People in Turkey, in general, do not view things from a racial standpoint. There is no "gene" of racism in Turks. Even a child of Turkish lineage may not know that he or she is a "Turk." However, as long as studies progress and the level of education increases, the Turks will certainly learn more, and on a larger scale, about themselves and their brothers in the world.

12. *What kind of significance does this have for the people of Turkey? Do you have anything to say about these studies and their relevance to Turkish-American relations?*

I have covered this in the previous question.

13. *Could these studies foster better Turkish-American relations? How?*

Certainly they can. All good relations in the world are built upon friendship. What improves humanity are relations based upon friendship. And what destroys it are relations built upon enmity. The Melungeons' endorsement of brotherhood and sisterhood with the Turkish people—even if only as friends—would bring great advantages to both nations. And it would provide the Melungeons with even more character and a deeper sense of identity.

4

Supplemental Materials

A Melungeon Looks at Turkey

by N. Brent Kennedy

[Published in English in *Turkish Times* and in Turkish in *TARIH* (*History*), Summer 1998.]

I admit I am in love with Turkey. With her people, her land, and much of her history. My wife has forgiven this indiscretion, for she knows I cannot help myself and she has consented to permit this other "woman" to coexist under our roof. I did not expect to fall in love. Yes, I knew prior to my first filming expedition that my people—the Melungeons (pronounced *muh-lun-junz*) of the Appalachian Mountains—were of probable Ottoman-Turkish and sixteenth-century Portuguese/Moorish origins. But I had also grown up in a society where evil was personified by the Moor, the Turk, the so-called infidel, and where Americans were told that the best that modern Turkey could offer was a society exemplified by the cruel but inept Turks of the 1960s blockbuster film, *Lawrence of Arabia*, or, more recently, a supposedly true film highlighting a wretchedly unfair Turkish system of justice called *Midnight Express*. But I was compelled by some inward spirit to go see for myself the theoretical homeland of at least some of my ancestors. My friends advised me not to go, and then when it was clear that I would ignore them and go anyway, they insisted that I at least get all possible inoculations and, under no circumstances, drink the water or venture out at night lest I be murdered by some crazed Muslim zealot. I did visit my physician and endured all sorts of needles and pills, and I slept not one second on the long trip from Atlanta to New York to Zurich to Rome and, finally, to Istanbul. (The reason for such an insane flight pattern is fodder for another story on another day!) But, when at long last I stepped off the plane, inexplicably all the doubts dissipated like a cloud of vapor. I could see it in the faces of the people who greeted me. In their physical features, their eyes, even their demeanor. I was home, and I knew it.

Three years and five more treks to Turkey later, not only the oral traditions among our people, but the genetics, the linguistics, and long-ignored historical archival records are substantiating the presence of Ottoman Turks, Portuguese, and other Mediterranean settlers in sixteenth-century Virginia and the Carolinas. They came as businessmen and traders to the colonies, textile workers and servants to both the English and the Spanish; and possibly some one hundred Levants were jettisoned as human cargo by Sir Francis Drake on the North Carolina coast in 1586. Unfortunate young men were enslaved by their Spanish captors after some long-forgotten Mediterranean battle and engaged in forced labor in the Caribbean (Cartagena) until Drake, by chance or maybe divine intervention, attacked the stronghold where they were kept. And though they undoubtedly wanted to return home, reunion with their loved ones was not their destiny. Instead, they were abandoned here, inter-married with Native Americans, and later again with Europeans, Africans, and others who arrived on these shores. They intermarried or otherwise took surnames like Kennedy, Nash, Mullins, Collins, Osborne, Goins, Hall, Ramsey, Alley, Reece, Sexton, and Moore, to name but a few. They did everything they could to blend in, for melding was the only way to survive. And amazingly, significant parts of their cultural and genetic nature survived as well, despite the overwhelming Anglo effort to stamp out every thread of evidence. It's why some of us Melungeons—supposedly just "dark" Englishmen—have sarcoidosis, thalassemia, Behçet's disease, familial Mediterranean fever, and Machado-Joseph disease. It's why we are lactose intolerant, have central Asian shovel teeth, the so-called "Turkish cranial bump," and Siberian cerumen. It's why 177 Melungeon blood samples analyzed by Dr. James Guthrie in a published gene-frequency study showed no significant differences between Melungeons and populations from the Galician Mountains of Portugal and Spain, Libya, Malta, Cyprus, the Levant coast, and northern Syria. (See appendix 5 for latest DNA findings.) It's why, during my first trip, people who didn't know I was an American addressed me in Turkish. And maybe it's also why hundreds of words from the Melungeons and related southeastern Native American tribes, have nearly identical counterparts in Ottoman-period Turkish: the old Melungeons called a watch a *saats*, the Cherokee word for "mother" or "woman" is *Ana-ta*, and the Cherokee word for "father" or "supreme chief" is *Atta*. The Creek Indian word for Holy Man is *Hadjo*, and our old folks thanked their cows and goats when milking them by saying "Sag" (pronounced "sow" in the Appalachian dialect). And the list goes on and on. Not all of these can be accidents and I, and other Melungeons, know that. Even our name, long a mystery to the Anglos, suddenly makes sense if one considers a possible Turkish and/or Arabic origin (and Ottoman Turkish was, of course, a blending of Turkish, Arabic, and Persian). For a people abandoned in a new and threatening world, never seeing their families again, denied the rights to vote, to go to school, to own land, or to hold a job, and ridiculed when trying to claim their true origin, the term *melun can*—"cursed soul" (and pronounced the same as "Melungeon" in both Turkish and Arabic)—needs no further explanation. Yes, my ancestors were indeed *meluncanlar*, regardless of their origins.

But the story need no longer be a sad one. There is a beautiful lesson here, a powerful message that God set into motion 400 years ago and is now, at long last, being delivered. What was a horrible story for those Ottoman immigrants has now turned into an inspired mission—a mission that would have been impossible had these sad circumstances never occurred. For today, we Melungeons can serve as the linkage between the Old and the New, the East and the West, the Parent and the Child. We Melungeons can serve as the glue to tie all people of Central Asian origin together. No longer does the Turkic story stop in the West at Istanbul or in the East in Siberia—instead, it spins its history across both the Bering Strait and the Atlantic Ocean, at last completely encircling the globe. This reality is not new, but the recent recognition of it is indeed staggering in its implications. And it begs for continued academic study and personal introspection. Such introspection has occupied much of my private time. And I believe some of my thoughts—thoughts mirrored by other Melungeons as well—should perhaps be shared with modern Turks. Not that we Melungeons know Turkey better than present-day Turks, nor do we, an ocean away, necessarily know what's best for Turkey. As Americans, we struggle like everyone else just to figure out what's best for our own nation. But we Melungeons do perhaps have a fresh view of Turkey—and Turks—that no other population on Earth possesses. We view Turkey as an orphaned child might view its mother or father after growing up alone and then enduring a lifelong journey to locate that missing parent. While we are proud Americans dedicated to our nation, we are also captivated by the prospects of reestablishing a family bond with our parent. What orphaned child doesn't dream of such a reunion? And it is this unique perspective from which I write.

So, as a Melungeon, what it is that I would say to a Turk in Turkey?

First, I would say that our histories are not so different, despite 400 years of separation. The Appalachian people in general have always been a rugged, independent, proud mountain people recognized for their indomitable spirit, their superior bravery and skill as soldiers, their skill as artisans, their family cohesiveness, and, yes, for their different culture when compared to other Euro-American populations. We have always been a people seemingly surrounded by enemies, disparaged, misunderstood, feared, and all the while alternately demanding and begging the outside world for acceptance. These characteristics have perhaps contributed to the self-sufficient nature of our Appalachian people. And, I believe, made us so much like the Turks who have suffered the same indignities. How wise of God, to separate us but still give us a common experience so that, even four centuries later, we are still culturally and psychologically the same people.

Second, I would also say to my Turkish brothers and sisters, that for we Melungeons who have struggled so hard to reclaim our heritage and our kinship, the thought of modern Turks taking for granted the ties that bind them together is inconceivable, even deplorable. Must you, like us, lose your sense of self before appreciating it? I always encourage those young Turkish students in the U.S.A. to study hard but to return home if possible and apply their skills and intellect to building a stronger Turkey. I feel like crying when I hear a young German whose mother is a Turk, deny his Turkish heritage. That is precisely what we did and for four centuries could not erase the high cost of denying our very selves. What has the past taught us? We Melungeons can teach a valuable lesson to all these young people of the terrible price when one is forced to surrender his or her identity to find acceptance. I implore my Turkish brothers and sisters to put aside any petty differences and to work together to build not only a stronger, more industrialized, and economically sound Turkey, but to remain committed to both democracy and universal human rights.

Third, it would appear to be time for a Central Asian confederation that not only celebrates across common borders its shared culture and heritage, but that is unequivocably dedicated to bettering the lives of its citizenry, especially the poor and disenfranchised. No single Turkish ethnic subgroup can be superior to another, nor to any other human group, and indeed this guarantee is the theoretical cornerstone of modern Turkish freedom. As an example, after 400 years of intermarriage, we Melungeons now share many diverse heritages, ranging from Ottoman Turks, Jews, and Moors, to Native Americans, Africans, and Europeans. Our original population has spread into all American racial and ethnic groups, so much so that our tribal creed is now "Melungeons: One People, All Colors." And this is our greatest strength as a population. Even Melungeons are Americans first, and then and only then, Melungeons. When Professor Türker Özdoğan and I attended the Turkic World Economic Congress in Izmir (at the invitation of Professor Turan Yazgan) last summer, I noted with delight that the various Turkic representatives came in all sizes, shapes, and colors. Whether their skin was a beautiful ebony shade, a lovely ivory cast, or a captivating olive or red, the pride of a Turkic heritage was always there. I met Muslim Turks, Christian Turks, Jewish Turks, Buddhist Turks, Shaman Turks, and just Turks. This Turkic kinship crosses all national, theological, and so-called ethnic and racial boundaries, with the key to membership lying not in physical phenotype but simply within the heart of each human being. I can tell you that here in America if one feels himself or herself to be a Melungeon and is willing to declare it publicly regardless of prejudices, then he or she is a Melungeon. Based on Atatürk's philosophy, I would assume as well that if one feels himself to be a Turk, then one is indeed a Turk, regardless of national origin or residence. And if this is indeed true, then the heart of "pan-Turkism" must correspondingly be "Turks: One People . . . Many Nations."

Fourth, related to the above, a nonmilitant and, importantly, nonnationalistic form of pan-Turkism is acceptable, even advisable given recent events. I recognize the challenges of unifying populations with well-defined common interests but complicated by well-defined national borders. It is possible for neighbors and friends to join hands and hearts in common cause without moving into the same house. Just as the European nations feel compelled to unite with others of like mind and culture, and the Latin world feels drawn to a Pan-American Union, and just as the Arab world longs for a similar union, so are Turkic peoples deserving of the same courtesy. Especially when the effort to be a part of another union has been repeatedly rebuffed. Like most Turks I, too, was praying that the European Union would welcome Turkey into its fold with open arms. I thought this would be good for Turkey both economically and politically. But that didn't happen, and frankly I don't think it is apt to happen, at least not in the unencumbered way that Turks would prefer. And now, as with my abandoned ancestors, I'm not so sure that divine providence didn't step in once again on Turkey's behalf. Most gifts from God must be suffered through before the real meaning and value is understood. I came to understand my heritage through a life-threatening illness, but in retrospect it was that very "misfortune" which led me to illumination. Turkey's rejection by the EU is Europe's loss, not Turkey's, and time will show this to be the case. But there is a wonderful gift clothed in this rejection, a gift well understood by most Melungeons. We frantically sought full assimilation and acceptance by early Anglo-Americans, but it never came. Or when it did come, it came only to those willing to suffer total loss of the former self. Amazingly, we nevertheless managed to survive as a somewhat intact culture and—four centuries later—are now reconnecting with our family. What seemed to be an utter and total rejection by those around us was instead a great gift from God. Turkey has just received such a gift. With an increased emphasis on Central Asian, Siberian, and Caucasian linkages, coupled with increasingly stronger bonds with the United States and Israel, the inevitable benefits that will accrue to Turkey will more than compensate for Europe's shortsightedness.

Fifth, and finally, we Melungeons are proud to possess Turkish heritage, just as we are proud of the blood of every other nationality or race that flows through our veins. For some of us, the Anglo genes have captured our spirits, for others the Native American, or the African-American, or simply the "American." And this is perfectly acceptable since we are unified by a common heritage and cultural origin, but liberated by the diversity that followed due to intermarriage as well as our individual freedom to celebrate whatever it may be about ourselves or our culture or our history that most pleases or intrigues us. For me, it is undeniable: I am a "cultural Turk," a blending of Central Asia and the Mediterranean. And I always have been a cultural Turk, even before I knew the truth of who I was genetically. My central Asian anthropological characteristics, as well as my sarcoidosis and familial Mediterranean fever, simply confirmed physically what I already knew spiritually. And there are others like me. Others who instinctively think in the same way as Turks, react to certain music and food in the same way, and cannot help but show our emotions even if it means embracing our dearest male friends in a most non-Anglo manner. This is who we are—and who we were—even before discovering the reasons why. Those Turks who have visited our small town have invariably commented on how much they felt at home. Of how similar our customs and our culture seemed to be. The undeniable connections are there. Blood is indeed thicker than water. And for many Melungeons, it is Turkish—that is, Central Asian and Mediterranean—blood that pulls us eastward.

Our journey of discovery is not yet finished and, indeed, is likely to never be totally completed. At least I hope not, for it is the journey that teaches us what we need to know: what it is to be a Melungeon, or a Turk, or a human being of any complexion or origin. By more fully understanding my own true origins, I not only feel my spiritual connectedness to Turks, but to every other human being, from Native Americans and Africans, to Arabs and Jews, to Greeks and Armenians. Being a "Melungeon" or a "Turk" means being a true citizen of the World, culturally and genetically, and thus we are spiritual siblings to *all* other human beings. To revisit the circumstances of those abandoned sixteenth-century Ottoman Levants, did not they themselves represent all creeds and colors but still were "Turks" nevertheless? And were they not sailing together under Barbarosa's remarkable flag of religious tolerance—a naval banner combining the Muslim Star and Crescent, the Christian Cross, and the Jewish Star of David? By once again recognizing this undeniable kinship are we not coming full circle to the time-worn truth that we are all God's children? If we are willing to hear it, the answer is yes. By discovering my Turkish roots, I am now, more than before, a human being whose kinship does—and indeed must—touch all other human beings. For me, it can be no other way. My mission is to ensure that the Melungeon story is told again and again, and that through its telling *all* people might learn something about their unseen human kinships, about kindness and mercy, and most certainly about justice. No injustice can be buried or ignored, whether committed upon or by a Melungeon, or upon or by a Turk. At some point every deed—good or bad—will see the light of day. Four hundred years and all the ethnic prejudice and racial laws our early republic could muster could not suppress the eventual telling of our story. It was the search for truth that brought me, and other Melungeons back to our roots and such searches will forever more be indispensible to us as a people. And it is this continuing search for truth that will pull Turks and Melungeons—and thus Turkey and the United States—even more closely together. I give thanks to God for permitting me to learn the truth about who I am, and for the wonderful friends He has brought my way, and for the challenges and tests He has used—and continues to use—to prod me along my path. I look forward to this continuing odyssey with the confidence that for both Melungeons and Turks a new dawn is at hand.

* | * | *

Acceptance Speech

by N. Brent Kennedy

[Acceptance of the ATAA Distinguished Service Award at the Assembly of Turkish American Associations Annual Banquet, Washington, D.C., October 10, 1998.]

Honored dignitaries, guests, friends:

What a marvelous honor you have bestowed on me. On behalf of all American Melungeons, thank you.

The journey of the Melungeon people, though 400 years old, is really only beginning. Denied our heritage, and even the God-given right to self-identify, the Melungeon people dispersed from the Southern Appalachians and spread throughout America, losing themselves in the great, and sometimes wonderful, American melting pot. And their descendants—including such icons as Abraham Lincoln and Elvis Presley—eventually "fit in" and melded with the primarily Anglo culture that surrounded them. But even after 400 years, small pockets of our people continue to remember—and proclaim—their remembered origins. My family is a good example. The old ones said they were variously Portuguese, or Jewish, and, yes, even Turkish. And the mysterious word "Melungeon"—pronounced "Muh-lun-jun"—was always associated with them. A word that turns out to be identical to the Turkish/Arabic *melun jinn* (*meluncan*), meaning "cursed soul." The term "Melungeon" itself turned out to be an intriguing piece of the evidence: what an appropriate self-description for a people who couldn't attend school, couldn't vote, couldn't own property, and could not step foot in a courtroom. A people often maligned, demeaned, and debased by their neighbors. My own great-grandfather was nearly beaten to death—and then later murdered—when he tried to vote in Coeburn, Virginia in the early 1900s. I myself remember the derogatory names applied to my mother's family.

But now we know who we are, and thanks to modern research methods and genetics, we can prove it. Major research initiatives are now underway, ranging from linguistics, to historical archival records, to medicine and genetics. Dr. Turan Yazgan and Professor Türker Özdoğan are, incidentally, key players in these research efforts, along with dozens of American scholars. The results to date are staggering. A few examples:

- Early British and American records indicate the strong likelihood that, in 1586, Sir Francis Drake likely set off on the North Carolina coast several hundred Turkish Levants and Moorish sailors, who later moved inland and intermarried with Native Americans.

- The sixteenth-century Spanish were bringing Kavkaz and Karachai Turks to the New World to operate their silk and textile industries.

- Seventeenth-century Virginia records show a strong Ottoman presence in Virginia, with Turkish businessmen and silk workers, as well as indentured servants, populating the early colony. So much so that Virginia enacted a law forbidding the importation of any more "Turks" and so-called "infidels" into the colony. But many were already here. And they stayed, survived, passing on their genes and their culture, though their true origins were eventually to be dismissed by Anglo historians as "myth."

But the evidence of their survival is all around us.

- Why did the Creek Indians wear fezzes and call their Holy man a Hadjo?
- Why did Cherokees dress identically to Levants, wear turbans, and call their chief, Atta Kulla Kulla?
- Why was the Cherokee word for father the same as Turkish (*atta*), and their word for womankind *ana-ta*?

And on and on and on.

On a more personal note: Why, when some historians, tell me that I am northern European, do I have a central Asian cranial ridge? And central Asian shovel teeth? And even more telling, familial Mediterranean fever, a genetically based, ethnically restricted disease, invariably found among Turks, Armenians, Druze, and non-Ashkenazi Jews? Why do members of my family also have Behçet's disease and thalassemia? This should be impossible if we are truly nothing more than Anglo.

How is that 177 Melungeon blood samples tested in a gene frequency study showed no significant differences between Tennessee and Virginia Melungeons, and populations in southern Portugal, north Africa, Malta, Cyprus, the Levant coast, northern Iraq, and northern Iran, the very parameters of the sixteenth-century Ottoman Empire. And exactly what we would expect, given the legends of our ancestors. Thank goodness for modern genetics, for while you can change a man's name and religion, you cannot so easily change his genes.

But what is the real importance of this story? Its relevance to today's world?

First, it confirms that the United States and Turkey share a history far more common than originally supposed. Many of us are indeed part "Turkish"—whether we are the more recently arrived Melungeons, such as myself, or Native Americans, some of whose ancestors migrated eastward and crossed the Bering Strait thousands of years earlier. There are those who don't want these stories known, but the truth is the truth. And understanding the truth can mean wondrous things for both Turkey and the United States.

Second, in this regard, it opens the door for a new dawn in Turkish-American relations. An enhanced relationship built not simply upon successful lobbying on behalf of Turkey as a trusted, strategically important ally, but more importantly, as a relative. Historically, doing business with Turkey has been marketed here at home as politically and strategically important despite our cultural and ethnic differences. That can, should, and must change. There are Americans here—*old* Americans—who possess, and are proud of, their Turkish origins. Turkish people played a role in the settling of this great nation. This represents a major shift in thinking, and should of necessity impact on how we go about the business of educating the American public.

Third, and perhaps most important, the Melungeon story teaches us that whether we realize it or not, we are indeed related to all other human beings. Young men and women growing up in the hills of Tennessee, or the mountains of Kentucky, or the bayous of Louisiana are not simply rural Americans invariably and exclusively tied to northern Europe, but Americans who are literally cousins to young men and women living their lives in Istanbul, Turkey, or Azerbaijan, or Cyprus, or Tel Aviv. The irony of unacknowledged central Asian, Middle Eastern, and Mediterranean genes and culture flowing westward during the early settlement of this nation should not be lost on those who wish to isolate the United States from world events, nor by those who wish to engage world events from what they perceive as our historically European perspective. It wasn't always that way.

In closing, my ten-year journey has led me to reevaluate my own perspective—and my own life. To educate myself to the point that today, even if I had no Turkish roots at all, I would still be a champion of improved Turkish-American relations. But to be candid, given the connection, the drive to do so is overwhelming. My life is now caught up with this passion to educate my countrymen and, for me, I'm afraid it's far too late to cease.

I am an American who deeply loves and respects his country. While the lives of my ancestors may have been less than perfect, I remain a proud American. And, again, I thank you for this award and hope that our two nations will continue to work closely together in creating a safer and better world.

* | * | *

DNA Study Answers and Raises Questions about the Melungeons

[General press release approved by Dr. Kevin Jones and the Melungeon Heritage Association prior to the Fourth Union, 2002.]

•**Kingsport, Tennessee, June 20, 2002** — Some of the veil of mystery surrounding the "mysterious" Melungeons was lifted today when the results of a two-year DNA study were announced. New questions have been raised, however, concerning females from Turkey and northern India who are a part of the Melungeon ancestry.

The Melungeons are a group of people of unknown origin first documented in the mountains of Appalachia in the early nineteenth century. Many believed they were of mixed racial ancestry and the Melungeons faced legal and social discrimination. As a result, they tended to live in remote areas, most notably Newman's Ridge in Hancock County, Tennessee. In the 1940s and 1950s, sociologists and anthropologists labeled the Melungeons and other similar groups as "triracial isolates."

Over the years, numerous myths, legends, and theories evolved to explain the Melungeons' mysterious origins. These legends often involved sailors and explorers from Spain, Portugal, Carthage, or Phoenicia who were stranded on the American continent and intermarried with Indians. The Melungeons themselves often claimed to be "Portyghee." Most researchers believed they were the product of intermarriage between English and Scots-Irish settlers, Indians, and free African-Americans, and discounted their claims of Mediterranean origin.

The DNA results announced today confirmed that the Melungeons have European, African, and Native American ancestry, as well as genetic similarities with populations in Turkey and northern India. More surprising, however, is the fact that some of these Turkish and northern Indian genes have been passed through the Melungeons' maternal lines, indicating that their overseas ancestors included not only male sailors and explorers, but females as well.

The results were announced today at Fourth Union, a Melungeon conference in Kingsport, Tennessee sponsored by the Melungeon Heritage Association (MHA). MHA is a nonprofit organization dedicated to promoting research and understanding about Melungeons and other multiracial groups in the United States. Dr. Kevin Jones, a biologist at the University of Virginia's College at Wise, conducted the study.

The presence of Turkish and northern Indian genes within the mitochondrial DNA samples taken from modern-day Melungeons indicates that women of European/Asian origin were a part of the original mixture that made up the Melungeon ancestry. Mitochondrial DNA comes from the female side of an individual's ancestry. Previous researchers had assumed that European males intermarried with Native Americans and African-Americans to produce the Melungeons. Although Native and African genes are definitely a part of the Melungeon genetic mix, women were among the overseas settlers who contributed to the Melungeon gene pool.

This finding indicates that the overseas ancestors of the Melungeons came to these shores as part of a male-female family unit, or formed such family units shortly after arrival. Such family units came to America as part of a Spanish/Portuguese colony at Santa Elena in present-day South Carolina.

Dr. N. Brent Kennedy speculated that the Melungeons were of Mediterranean and Middle Eastern ancestry and published his theories in a book entitled *The Melungeons: The Resurrection of a Proud People*, published in 1994 by Mercer University Press.

Dr. Jones, a native of London, England, studied at the University of Reading, and did postdoctoral research at Louisiana State University. He is currently a professor of biology at UVA-Wise, teaching courses including cell biology and genetics. Dr. Jones undertook this DNA study in 2000 at the suggestion of Dr. Kennedy, then vice-chancellor at the University of Virginia's College at Wise. Kennedy asked Jones to analyze DNA samples taken from members of known Melungeon families. Such a study would utilize technology not available to earlier researchers.

"Brent Kennedy . . . explained the controversy that surrounded the origins of the Melungeons [and] realized that I had the DNA expertise to look at that," Jones related in an interview with Wayne Winkler, president of the Melungeon Heritage Association and author of an upcoming book about the Melungeons. "The subjects were largely chosen by Brent Kennedy on the basis of pursuing as many of the known Melungeon lineages that existed in the area and taking advantage of his genealogical expertise. People were then asked to donate samples to the study, and in the majority of cases they kindly did so." Kennedy worked directly with respected members of the east Tennessee and southwest Virginia Melungeon communities to collect samples representing the oldest Melungeon families.

Single hairs were taken to study the mitochondrial DNA which traces the maternal lines of the subject. In other words, the samples represented DNA, which could be traced to the subject's mother, grandmother, great-grandmother, and so on. "We also have a smaller number of samples which are cheek cells for looking at male inheritance," said Jones.

"What we get from those is a DNA sequence which we can think of as being about an 800-long letter code, and we can take that string of 800 letters and compare those to what now is literally thousands of samples from around the world. We're interested both in the number of different sequences that we get from the population and also how they appear to relate to other samples worldwide."

About 120 hair samples were studied for mitochondrial, or maternal, DNA, and about forty samples of cheek cells were taken to study the Y chromosome, or male, DNA. While more samples might have been taken, Jones said, "That's the beauty of science: one can always repeat and extend the analysis." The technology available to Jones allowed him to study only the mitochondrial DNA samples; the Y chromosome samples were sent to University College in London, England, for study. "The 'Y' is technically far harder to do, and indeed, relies on expertise in some other labs in the world to do it, so we're partly dependent on their cooperation and collaboration."

Such testing is not perfect, of course, and does not tell researchers everything about an individual's inheritance. For example, neither test will give genetic information about a subject's paternal grandmother. However, the study was not particularly concerned with individual results. "We're looking for patterns that exist in the population as a whole," according to Jones. "Now, obviously, each individual sample contributes to that, but I think that for an individual you can say relatively little. Looking at the patterns that occur throughout the population becomes important. And that means the number of samples that are looked at is also significant, and we've tried to do as many as is reasonably possible."

Jones compared these samples to the thousands available through GenBank, an international genetics database, and the Mitochondrial DNA Concordance, databases containing DNA sequence information. Looking at the maternal lines of the Melungeons who were tested, Jones found considerable variation in ethnicity among the samples. "It's comparatively straightforward to link particular sequences to particular ethnic groups and different areas of the world," he noted, "and the majority of those Melungeon-derived sequences were European in origin. Within those European samples, though, there is an awful lot of diversity, and some seem to reflect areas outside the traditional northern European sphere.

"The ability to tie a sequence to a particular area is dependent upon the historical occurrence of any given sequence somewhere, and the places that are easy to track are where we've had populations existing for a long time, and not being affected by a lot of different people coming in. So some, perhaps more isolated, areas of Europe are easier to track than more cosmopolitan [areas]."

While the Melungeons are predominantly European in their genetic backgrounds, they are indeed triracial. "There appears to be a small percentage of both Native American and African-American sequences in there, too," Jones stated, "although they are certainly both in the minority. They're both in there in about equal levels of representation as well."

The long-held belief that the Melungeons originated in Portugal is neither borne out nor negated by Jones's research. "To date we've found no sequences that can be definitively traced back to uniquely Portuguese sequences. That doesn't mean that they don't exist. A large number of the European sequences are now widely spread throughout Europe, and if one of those genetic sequences happened to come from Portugal we would not detect that. We can't dismiss that theory at the moment, but we can't provide additional support for it."

Jones finds a stronger possibility for a Turkish or Middle Eastern ancestry for the Melungeons. "The relatively unusual European-type sequences seem to reflect, perhaps, areas around northern India. It's very hard to say, back in time, what that would have been classified as, and I think one of the problems here is that we tend to think of 'Turkish' in terms of the dimensions of modern Turkey, not of the original scale of people of Turkish origin who, in essence, were spread throughout the European world. Perhaps the best I can say is that some of those sequences are a little more 'exotic' than Anglo-Irish sequences, and some of those could reflect, perhaps, populations that were associated with or moved through Turkey."

The Portuguese and Spanish explorers and early American settlers may well be the key to discovering how these people wound up in America. The Portuguese, in particular, were involved in wide-ranging trade in the fifteenth and sixteenth centuries, and had many interests in places such as northern India and the area occupied by present-day Turkey. Both Spain and Portugal had very cosmopolitan populations, with large numbers of people from many parts of the world living within their borders. And Dr. Kennedy and others have suggested the Spanish and Portuguese fort at Santa Elena (in present-day South Carolina), along with a series of frontier outposts, as a possible source for Melungeon ancestry.

Theories about when people with this genetic background first came to America are speculative at this point. "Dr. Jones's work has answered many questions," said Wayne Winkler, president of MHA, "but those answers have raised many more questions. These questions will keep historians busy for some time to come, and we may never have definite answers. The Melungeons may remain one of the mysteries of history."

* | * | *

The World Really Was Their Home

[Editorial by Stephen Phelps, opinion page editor, in the *Bristol Herald Courier*, June 23, 2002, page 6A—local daily newspaper serving East Tennessee and Southwest Virginia.]

Actually, family trees are more like puzzles. They may grow on their own, but to see them in all their glory you have to put them together yourself. And that's hard enough when you have all the pieces in front of you. So you can imagine what it's like for the Melungeons of Southwest Virginia and Northeast Tennessee. Not only are a lot of the pieces missing, but there's no telling what the puzzle will look like when it's finished, if ever. But for many of us with Melungeon ancestry, sorting through the pieces is proving to be well worth the effort. Last week at Fourth Union, a yearly Melungeon gathering being held in Kingsport this year, the latest piece was unveiled—results from DNA tests of Melungeons from Southwest Virginia and East Tennessee.

Alone, those results won't solve the puzzle. But they hint at a clearer understanding of who the Melungeons are and where they came from. And viewed from the proper angle, they even might offer a world of insight about our future. In fact, the Melungeons have been one of the Mountain Empire's [that is, essentially, Northeast Tennessee and Southwest Virginia] great puzzles for years, even centuries. With dark, distinctive looks and mysterious origins, the Melungeons of yesterday tended to live their lives apart, on the outside. And all too often, it was easier for them that way.

It's hard to think of many minority groups that don't suffer in some way, from stereotyping to outright persecution. For the Melungeons, the latter reached its peak in the person of W. A. Plecker, Virginia's commissioner of vital statistics in the first half of the twentieth century—an apostle of eugenics and racial purity who crusaded for decades to track down and single out Virginians of mixed race. With white, black, Native American, and other antecedents, Melungeons were among those who paid with their land, their civil rights and more.

Plecker tried to enlist school boards and county clerks in his effort; many, to their credit, refused. Yet during Plecker's reign of terror and long before, many Melungeons sought to conceal their origins—destroying papers, changing names, and often fleeing the region altogether. That has a lot to do with why our family trees often stop abruptly and tend to be more of a puzzle than most. And it's why a lot of folks out there have Melungeon ancestors and don't know it, or are just now finding out. It was just four years ago, in fact, that I learned I may actually be of Melungeon descent on both sides of my family.

I have no stories to tell about my Melungeon ancestors, not the way I can tell you about my forebears who sailed from Dublin to America in the late 1600s in a boat they built themselves. The DNA results unveiled this week for Fourth Union may not tell that kind of story, but the genetic evidence helps to highlight a fascinating, even inspiring, picture that's become gradually clearer in recent years.

For years, researchers and others assumed that the Melungeons were simply "triracial"—white, black, and Native American. More recently, it's begun to appear there's a lot more to it. In his book, *The Melungeons: The Resurrection of a Proud People*, Brent Kennedy suggests there were other factors in the genetic mix: shipwrecked Turkish sailors may have migrated inland to Central Appalachia in the 1500s and intermarried with those already here. Kennedy and others have suggested that Spanish and Portuguese settlers may also have wound up in the area. The DNA results, involving hair samples from 100 women in Southwest Virginia and Northeast Tennessee, indeed showed genetic patterns characteristic of whites, blacks, and Native Americans, according to Kevin Jones, a biology professor at The University of Virginia's College at Wise. But they showed something else as well: genetic strains often found in Turkey and northern India. What's more, they suggest that those strains were passed through the female line; in other words, those early pioneers were both men and women.

Obviously, last week's results are just a beginning. There will be other Melungeon genetic studies, probably many more. One truth, however, seems self-evident: This world really is the Melungeons' home, and not just the Mountain Empire, either. If it hadn't been for people from all over the world—Europe, the Mediterranean, the Middle East, Africa, Asia—converging in one place at a certain time in history, the Melungeons would not exist as a people. And if you believe in destiny, you have to conclude that those varied peoples converged here for a reason.

It should go without saying that the Melungeon experience could teach us all a lot about race relations and as I've often said, if you don't think that's still an issue in twenty-first century America, you probably need to pay closer attention. But then, it's not just America. What's struck me most, in fact, has been the growing bond between the Mountain Empire and Turkey. The town of Wise has a sister-city relationship with one Turkish city [Çeşme]; UVa-Wise has established exchange programs with Turkish universities; a surprising number of Southwest Virginians and Northeast Tennesseeans have traveled to Turkey, some repeatedly. A number have even spoken of feeling immediately at home there, and it's no small wonder: according to Kennedy, parts of Asia Minor bear a striking resemblance to the Powell Valley [in extreme southwest Virginia]. And when a massive earthquake struck Turkey three years ago, the people of this region—Melungeon and non-Melungeon alike—pitched in to help, donating money and organizing relief shipments. One youngster even used her birthday party to raise aid for quake victims.

In the past, the Mountain Empire has often tended to look inward; in a world where everything from fast food to terrorism has become global in scope, that's no longer an option. The Melungeon experience could inspire us all to look outward, and it might even help us piece together a puzzle or two.

* | * | *

A New *Path*

by N. Brent Kennedy

[A statement from Brent Kennedy, based on a speech to Fourth Union, the Melungeon Gathering, and later released to various websites and news outlets, June 24, 2002.]

The long-awaited DNA results are in and as many of us have maintained, the Melungeons are indeed a mixture of all races and many ethnic groups. The DNA samples in this study represent the oldest, most established Melungeon male and female lines in the Hancock County community, and the Wise County community. Extensive genealogies for these two populations—and those sampled—are known and documented. Respected members of each community assisted in the collection of the samples, and these samples can be examined separately (by community) and compared against one another.

In addition to Native American (approximately five percent of the sample), African (approximately five percent), and European/Eurasian (approximately eighty-three percent of the sample, but representing Europeans from north to south), the study also showed approximately seven percent of the samples matching populations in Turkey, Syria, and northern India. In other words, the surviving genes from Middle Eastern and East Indian ancestors are in equal proportion to those of Native Americans and Africans. My gut feeling is that the original, seventeenth-century percentages of all three groups (that is, African, Native American, and Middle Eastern/East Indian) were higher than what we're seeing today. Time, admixture, and out-movement of some of our darker cousins into other minority groups have likely lowered the genetic traces of their earlier presence. But enough of them were there to still be traceable among the Melungeons of today. The long discounted Mediterranean and Middle Eastern heritages are irrefutably there.

Very importantly, this study is only a sampling. It's impossible to get to every single bona fide Melungeon descendant. Consequently, all this— or any other—DNA study can do is *confirm* heritages—it cannot dismiss them. But via the genetic sequences found, it can give us a hint at the ethnic makeup of the earliest Melungeons. In this regard, I am still keeping an open mind regarding the theories that are out there. Four hundred years has allowed a great deal of time for population admixture and each family has its own distinct cultural and ethnic legacy. The original people referred to as Melungeons may have been Africans, or East Indians, or Native Americans, or Turks, or Gypsies or Portuguese, or whatever. Not one of us knows with absolute certainty. What we do know is that very early on these various populations combined into one people known as Melungeons.

As those who attended Fourth Union heard, from both Dr. Jones and Dr. Morris, this finding is incredibly important from a healthcare standpoint alone. Native Americans, Europeans, and African Americans can—and do—carry Middle Eastern and Mediterranean diseases. It takes very few individuals in a founding population to have a dramatic impact on a gene pool. African Americans and Native Americans can—and do—have familial Mediterranean fever. White Americans can—and do—have Sickle Cell Anemia. Having the genetic and genealogical data to explain why is critical to improving healthcare.

The study also underscores another important aspect of the origins debate: nearly all theories are correct to some extent. The only ones wrong are those that have been exclusive in their premise. The long-standing academic position that Melungeons are "triracial isolates" consisting of strictly northern Europeans, West Africans, and Native Americans is incorrect. Those unwilling to add any other ethnic group to the mix have been wrong. This is what I stated in my book and have maintained for years: we are mixed and highly inclusive, and that inclusiveness includes Mediterranean, Middle Eastern, and East Indian.

We should also keep in mind that these non-Native-American ethnic groups could have arrived in a myriad of ways, and likely did. Those who have read my book or heard me speak know that this has always been my position. I have never been wed to any theory of arrival—what I have been wed to is, simply, arrival. Santa Elena and its outlying forts continue to help explain how some of these people—and their genes— might have gotten here. There were Gypsies and Conversos (for example, Jews, Arabs, Berbers, East Indians, Turks, Moors, Africans, etc.) at Santa Elena who, even as "good Catholic Spaniards" and "good Catholic Portuguese" would have carried their ancestral genes from their ancestral homelands. The finding of Turkish genes (both male and female lines) in the Melungeon population seems to indicate full families, so Santa Elena remains an origin possibility for some of the Melungeon ancestors. There were no women with Drake's Turks and the Turks themselves weren't sending families here, at least as far as I know. The British, however, were doing so. Turkish and Armenian families were documentably present in Jamestown, serving the English colonists as indentured servants and artisans. Whatever the case, historians are best equipped to determine *how* the genes arrived. Finally, East Indians were brought to these shores in significant numbers from the early 1600s on and Romany (Gypsies) are also well documented in Virginia and the Carolinas during the same time period. There was, simply said, no shortage of the people necessary to provide the genetic proof to back up the Melungeon claims of origin.

I don't yet know my full family DNA results but when I do I, and hopefully others, will share the information in an effort to help solve the roles specific families have played in the Melungeon odyssey. But I do know one sequence and this single piece of information is enlightening. The mitochondrial DNA (mtDNA) of my mother's great-aunt, a heritage I likewise possess, is common to the Siddis of India. The dark-skinned Siddis likely originated from what today is Ethiopia, Eritrea, or Somalia—sub-Saharan East Africa. They were transported to India in a variety of ways, most not so pleasant, and formed a major component of what became known as the Untouchable Caste. Their lives—and the life of my ancestral mother—must have been horribly difficult. But she survived long enough to have at least one daughter and that daughter did likewise. And generation after generation this original Ethiopian girl's DNA was passed along until, in 1950, it came to my immediate family.

How my particular East Indian ancestor made her way to America remains unclear. It may have been as the wife of a sixteenth-century New World Portuguese settler (the sixteenth-century Portuguese soldiers married northern Indian women by the thousands). Or she may have been the spouse of a seventeenth-century British ex-patriot, or an East Indian female sent to the Caribbean as an indentured servant. Still again, she may have arrived on these shores as a Rom (or so-called Gypsy) girl. Many Romany share the Asian Indian mitochondria and the Romany-related surnames that follow this particular mitochondrial line in my family (Mullins, Bennett, Rose, etc.) would seem supportive of a Romany origin. Regardless of her mode of arrival to the New World, what is clear is that she—and her genes—did indeed make their way here. My mother and I are living proof of this woman's legacy. All this is to say that had a young, sub-Saharan East African girl never lived, never been transported to India, and never had a daughter of her own, I wouldn't be here.

So, what is the meaning of all this? For me, I can sum it up this way:

While I am likely—and proudly—of northern European heritage, I am also likely of Siddi heritage. And I am equally kin to the Scotsman tilling his field outside Glasgow, the Chickahominy Indian fighting to keep tribal pride alive, and the various East Africans at one another's throats in Somalia. The Israelis and Palestinians dealing out death on a daily basis, the Appalachian bluegrass banjo picker, the Indian and Pakistani soldiers staring one another down in Kashmir, and, yes, the downbeaten untouchable in the poorest ghettos of southern India are also family. All are literally, not just figuratively, *my* people. Genocide in the Balkans, earthquakes in Turkey, riots in Argentina, and repressive regimes in Afghanistan are no longer faraway occurrences of little consequence. In every tragedy on this earth, a relative is suffering. And this leads me to a deeper understanding of just what the Melungeon story really means, and the transition that I must make.

We in Appalachia are known for our powerful storytelling tradition. Beginning today we have the opportunity to tell the most important story in our history—the story of the oneness of humankind and how this oneness is exemplified in the Appalachian heartland. The irony that we in Appalachia and those whose roots lie in these mountains—long considered the lowliest of the low—could play a role in world ethnic harmony is staggering in its implications. But it's not a pipe dream. We can send a powerful message to all people everywhere, that:

> *No place, no region, no human being is too small, too remote, or too insignificant to justify dismissal. We are all of the same flesh and each of us matters.*

From this point on, our mission lies in spreading this message beyond these mountains. And we need to start at the earliest levels of teaching—our elementary schools—well before the seeds of racism and hate have been sown.

Beginning this week, I commit myself to this mission. The time has come for me to leave the historical and origins research, further DNA analysis, and other academic pursuits to those more qualified. My task was to be a catalyst—an instigator. Fourteen years ago, very few people cared about the Melungeons or any other mixed-race population for that matter. That deeply bothered me, as I felt that these various populations deserved more attention from academia and, indeed, had played a far larger role in building this nation than they'd ever been given credit for.

Placing them all into a box labeled "triracial isolate" and closing the lid seemed a grave injustice. I wrote my book to force the acknowledgement of our multiracial communities and, in a sense, to help bring them out of the closet in which academia had shoved them. I believe I've contributed to an increased awareness and, hopefully, an increased pride. The level of interest and the sheer volume of books and articles being written today is enormous compared to the late 1980s and early 1990s. This was my dream and I am now confident that this interest will not dissipate.

There are a myriad of talented researchers exploring a variety of Melungeon-related issues. Dozens of younger scholars are joining the older established writers and researchers in the search for Melungeon origins and the meaning of that search. Over the past decade, people like Jack Goins, Manuel Mira, Eloy Gallegos, James Nickens, Pat Elder, Mike Nassau, Wayne Winkler, Tim Hashaw, Carroll and Betty Goyne, Beth Hirschman, Joanne Pezzullo, Dennis Maggard, Karlton Douglas, Virginia DeMarce, Penny Ferguson, and Nancy Morison have added substantial knowledge to what we might soon begin calling "Melungeon Studies."[1] Each of these individuals deserves our gratitude and our praise. My long-standing hope has been, and continues to be, that all those researching this important topic can somehow pull together. That we acknowledge our differing opinions on historical matters, but that we come to recognize our shared commitment to (1) caring for these people and their culture and (2) abhorring racism in any form. These shared commitments far outweigh the debate over who showed up first, where the name came from, or what color John Doe might have been. Perhaps my greatest disappointment over the years has been the inability or unwillingness of what should have been fellow travelers on a very bumpy road to travel together. It's not too late.

In closing, I've done all I can do for those who came before us. From this point on, I plan on devoting my efforts to making this earth a better place for the living. If I've learned anything in this almost fifteen-year journey, it's the sobering reality that human prejudice exists everywhere—even within the very groups that have been the target of

---

[1]This list of acknowledgments is more extensive than that in the original text, but it is only fair to add the names of others who have exerted a significant impact on Melungeon studies during the two years since delivery of this address.

such prejudice. The heated debates over who can—or cannot be—a Melungeon are reminiscent of the earlier debates over who can—or cannot be—white. I know we don't intend it to be this way, but this is what invariably happens when we humans insist on categorizing and refining human ethnicity. It's this same mindset that, when carried to an extreme, results in prejudice, ethnic cleansing and, ultimately, genocide. "Race" is cultural, not genetic. I've been accused time and again of "diluting" Melungeon ethnicity to the point of blurring the boundaries and, in the words of one critic, "making them related to everybody." This is precisely what I intended to do and the DNA study results have supported this contention. That's the underlying beauty of this story, and to miss that point is symptomatic of the too-narrow focus that inevitably leads to ethnic tensions.

And so, what energy and time I have left will be expended in bringing people together wherever and whenever I can. In teaching and engaging in projects that can impact how human beings—and especially our children—view their fellow human beings: that we are not just figuratively—but literally—one human family. From Africa and India, to Turkey, Portugal, and the United States of America, we are one race. Where I can make a difference in helping others to understand this, I will. Where I cannot, I'll try.

And I pledge to live by our Melungeon creed, "One People, All Colors."

I thank God for an amazing fourteen years of chapter 1 and, God-willing, at least that many more for chapter 2.

The Last Chapter of the Book

Joseph M. Scolnick, Jr.

No genuine conclusion for this book is possible. The processes of action and interaction discussed in these pages are continuing as this is being written and appear likely to continue and even expand beyond their present dimensions. Furthermore, all of the persons interviewed here are alive, quite vigorous, and going about their affairs. So there is no true "end" to discuss. Rather, as stated above, this is simply the book's last chapter, an interview with myself. What this chapter will do is to permit a person who has played a part in the Turkish-Melungeon connection, to make some remarks about the subject, attempt to focus on several points that need further emphasis, tie together a few loose ends, and give a temporary goodbye to the subject. For reasons of stylistic unity and read-ability, it is in the form of a questionnaire that I will answer in conversational language.

1. *When did you first hear about the Melungeons? What were your initial reactions to the information you received about them?*

Although I had lived in Southwestern Virginia for more than two decades, I do not recall ever having heard about people called "Melungeons" until Brent Kennedy told me about them during a lunch we had at a local restaurant in, I believe, the fall of 1997. What I heard sounded entirely possible although conclusive evidence was not available for it at that time.

The basic story has three parts. The first is that the French, Spanish, and Portuguese had people of Eastern Mediterranean "blood" among them in the fifteenth to eighteenth centuries. Well, that was a given. There was a huge amount of mixing of peoples in the Mediterranean starting long before there were nation-states and nationalities. The second part is that, during those centuries, the French, Spanish, and Portuguese had sent ships that visited what became the southeastern United States. Again, that seemed obvious to me. There had been no large-scale, successful colonization of the area by those countries, but visits by their ships—in fact, quite a few visits—were a distinct possibility. So the first two parts were not only possible, but even rather likely.

The third part is that people from these ships, for a variety of reasons, had been left in the southeastern U.S. and somehow had managed to be accepted by tribes of Native Americans in the area and, thus, left offspring. This would be the most difficult part to actually prove but it certainly could have occurred. It does not stretch the imagination very much to visualize that, after all. If we know anything about the human species, it is that large numbers of our ancestors have been moving around on the earth at least since we have records of them and that many individuals and groups have been incredibly resourceful and tenacious in surviving, and even thriving, in the face of seemingly impossible situations. So, no, there was nothing impossible about the story. It would just take a sustained effort to show to what extent the story Brent Kennedy told had occurred in fact.

In short, I readily accepted the Melungeon "thesis" as a complex but interesting question for continuing research that well could have a factual basis. However, determining that in a convincing manner would be the chief difficulty.

2. How strong do you think the evidence is about the Melungeons? What work remains to be done in further identifying their origins?

There are two questions here. Let's take them one at a time.

First, the evidence about the Melungeons is not conclusive but it is fairly strong that peoples of Mediterranean background were living in the southeastern U.S. by the first decades of the seventeenth century. How and when they arrived and how they lived after their arrival has not been conclusively shown. There are diverse types of evidence but the study of these varied pieces is mostly in its very early stages. It is a long way from presenting a convincing picture. So there are decades of work to be done in many fields for people who have an interest in doing it. I won't comment on what they might find. I just don't know.

What has been shown by at least decent evidence is that the picture portrayed by the history books of the people of this region of the U.S. is definitely erroneous. Affairs were considerably more complex than they have been portrayed. Thus, the old picture is almost certainly wrong, yet there is insufficient evidence to convincingly state just what did occur. This should come as no surprise. What we have here are some very interesting questions to explore. So there is a conflict now between two pictures of some of the peoples of the southeastern Atlantic region of the U.S., the old one being very likely incorrect while a newer, more complex picture remains far from being complete and generally convincing. If I were a betting man, I would definitely put my money on some variation of the Melungeon story as being closer to the facts than the traditional picture.

Now for the second part of the question: What needs to be done? A great deal! This is such a complex subject and every part of it needs further examination. It is far too varied a subject for research to go over in any detail here, even if I could. It must involve more than a dozen fields of academic study. Moreover, there badly needs to be some organization created and funded that will keep track of the relevant ongoing research in the different fields and tie it together. It also would be very useful if this organization had funds both to spur new, promising lines of study and the capacity to ensure that the most interesting research results were appropriately publicized. But the funding, creation, and operation of a Melungeon studies organization surely would be a major undertaking and well out my areas of expertise.

3. *Do you believe you are yourself of Melungeon background? How do you feel about this?*

Based on what I know about both sides of my family, I consider it highly unlikely that I am a Melungeon. When I was in Turkey on three occasions with Brent Kennedy and other Melungeons, I would sometimes be asked if I was a Melungeon and my answer was always that I was "a friend of Brent Kennedy." My parents were both from Norfolk, Virginia, but, during the Great Depression and before I was born, they moved to Long Island. My father's family came to the U.S. in the late nineteenth century. My mother's family came to the U.S. in 1664 and settled in the Yorktown, Virginia area. So it is possible, but not very likely, that I could be of Melungeon descent on my mother's side.

How would I feel about it? Since my family is already highly diverse in its origins, this would just be adding another piece to the mix for me. Now it is certainly possible that some of my ancestors on my father's side lived in the Ottoman Empire at one time or another. It wouldn't surprise or disturb me in the least to learn that but I have no solid reason to believe it is so. Unlike Southwest Virginia where I live now, I grew up in an extremely diverse ethnic, racial, and religious part of the country. The Melungeons would just have been another small group and probably would have gone unnoticed had they originated there. Furthermore, even if it were shown that I was a Melungeon, it obviously would not mean the same to me as, for example, to the folks interviewed in this book.

4. *How would you define or describe Melungeons?*

As an overall description, I would say that they are a combination of "Caucasian," Native American, and "Blacks" in widely varying combinations while also having some Mediterranean "blood." They will never be easily described or precisely defined. And this is just one of the reasons why they will never become a cohesive, powerful interest group of some sort. They aren't *just* Melungeons; they are many things, such as Americans, Baptists, and so on that for most of the people on most occasions will be more important than their being Melungeon. Still, the Melungeon aspect of their ancestry will matter a good deal for some of them.

5. *What is the significance of the Melungeon story in general?*

This is difficult for me to answer. I do not think about it very much. One reason is simply because it touches on so many things. Which of them will be the most important in the future is more than I care to predict. But let me make a few points.

a. Given the history of the Melungeons of the southeastern U.S., gaining a better, truer sense of their ancestry is important for many of them. They understand far better now what occurred and why, and how their ancestors fitted into the scheme of things. They have learned more about their families and the people they knew and loved. And they can pass this sense of identity and self-value on to their children. The dark cloud of mystery has cleared to some extent for them. The past will not repeat itself.

b. It has critical medical importance for Melungeons, literally a matter of life and death. Now they stand a chance that many of their genetic-linked illnesses will be properly diagnosed and treated. The importance of this cannot be overemphasized.

c. They meet others who have had unfortunate experiences similar to theirs. This gives them a particular sense of belonging, of giving and receiving appreciation and respect.

d. They know more fully now that they are a part of the stories of the human race and of America that are still unfolding. These stories began many centuries ago but all are still working their way out. Each person has his or her role to play in not only the expansion of knowledge but in improving the behavior of peoples toward each other.

e. Many Melungeons are also learning a good deal about aspects of history, geography, non-American cultures, and so forth that they formerly knew next-to-nothing about. They are learning about other peoples and sometimes even meeting them. These people may well be their "kin" in some ways. Their worlds are quite literally expanding, especially if being Melungeon encourages them to travel abroad.

Who can possibly say where it will all lead? It is a grand story. Perhaps some day a truly inspired writer will put most of this together in a memorable story based on solid facts that hundreds of millions of people can identify with. I sense that the pieces are there.

6. *What is the personal significance of the Melungeon story to you?*

It may sound strange based on all I've said so far but it hasn't added a lot that is really new for me. I would say that it has amplified a number of preexisting themes in my life. I suppose the newest element is my interest in Turkey. My primary academic field is international politics. I had been interested in southern Europe (especially Spain and Italy) for many years but Turkey had never been part of that for me. In spite of holding three academic degrees and being a senior professor, I still had encountered virtually nothing about the Byzantine and Ottoman Empires and the Republic of Turkey. Now Turkish foreign policy is one of my major scholarly interests. There are a number of aspects that have aroused my interest. Furthermore, my college is a sister institution of Istanbul and Dumlupinar universities in Turkey and I very much want to ensure that these contacts are strengthened.

7. *What do you think of the likelihood of the possible connection between the Ottoman-Turkish people and Native American tribes?*

I must start by noting that I am aware of hardly anyone who would make this as a general proposition. To the extent there is a link, it is with a limited number of Native American tribes of the southeastern U.S. What is its probability even in this more limited context? Well, it is certainly not impossible. I know some highly intelligent, serious people who believe there is probably a link but openly acknowledge that quite inadequate evidence exists at present to strongly support the idea. Rather, what we have are bits and pieces all over the landscape, so to speak, that suggest a link with a half-dozen or so tribes, but that is about the most that can be said. The big question to me is less the existence or exact nature of the link than whether it will be viewed as a worthy, interesting subject for careful, extended study. I rather guess that it will receive less attention, at least for a while, than the Ottoman/Turkish/Melungeon connection. But it interests me personally to some extent. I have a strong sense that there are many more connections among peoples and groups than any of us were brought up to believe were true. How groups of humans have moved around the earth and adapted well or poorly to changed circumstances strikes me as an extremely interesting, important matter. In short, how did we all get where we live? For example, where were my family ancestors 500 or 2,000 years ago? For that matter, where were they 5,000 or 10,000 years ago? I may be directly linked to peoples with whom I would never imagine having any ties.

To what extent would these ties matter to me if I knew about them? That is also another interesting question I don't have an answer for.

8. What needs to be done, say, in the next five to ten years, to further establish on an empirical basis the Ottoman/Turkish—Native American connection.

The simple answer is that people must work on this question in a number of different ways and then communicate what they find to each other and to the broader public. I'm not going to try to provide an answer to what this would take in terms of human and material resources. I guess the chief question for me is the extent to which the possible linkage inspires people to undertake work on aspects of it. I think it highly likely that most of the work would be piecemeal. Capable scholars in many fields won't touch the subject unless some of what they find will be published. There has to be an outlet for their studies. Some people who take up an aspect of the subject will be complete amateurs who really don't understand what they are doing. Of course, some amateurs will make genuine contributions but they also will have to have what they have found published for others to learn of it. And those interested in different aspects of the subject must communicate with each other. It isn't an impossible task but it presents some formidable challenges. Again, the question for me is how strongly do people desire to explore this possible link? I'd like to think this book might interest people in this subject.

9. *How strong do you think is the evidence showing there is an Ottoman/Turkish-Melungeon connection?*

Although it is not conclusive yet, there is a good deal of evidence that supports to some extent a number of the elements of the basic Melungeon story. Furthermore, there is a quite a bit of interest in the story and people are tackling different aspects of it. So I expect a goodly amount more will be learned in the next five to ten years with some aspects strengthened, some weakened, and new lines of inquiry established. As a subject for serious study, it has probably reached a point where work on it is not going to fade anytime soon. But as I've already stated, there probably needs to be an umbrella organization to help encourage and coordinate the studies to some extent.

But what about the specific Ottoman/Turkish-Melungeon connection? There is some evidence that supports that link but it is not as strong as for some of the other parts of the Melungeon story. But, first off, it really must be stated that some Melungeons and quite a lot of Turks take the likelihood of the connection as a most serious subject. The extent to which this is true would surprise the American people. The people of the region where I live hardly understand it at all. Let me say a bit here about some personal experiences that relate to this matter.

In the summers of 1998, 1999, and 2000, I visited Turkey with Brent Kennedy and groups of Melungeons. I did this primarily as a colleague of Brent's at the University of Virginia's College at Wise and not as a Melungeon. Brent is treated almost as a hero in Turkey and certainly as a celebrity there. I recall one time when he spoke to a standing-room-only audience in a large auditorium in Kutahya and received fervent applause at the end of his talk. When the news media became aware of his presence in a town or city, he would be besieged for newspaper and television interviews. On several occasions while we were shopping together, Turks came out of their stores to tell him that they recognized him as the American Melungeon and shake his hand. Once on a trip from Ankara to Mersin, everyone on our bus had to stay and have tea when the owner of the service station where the bus was taking on fuel learned that the Melungeons were at his station. In Cesme, a "Melungeon Mountain" overlooks the harbor. All of the Melungeon visitors there have little pine trees planted on the mountain with their names on the tag. (There is one for me, too, although I'm not a Melungeon. Being a friend of Brent Kennedy in Turkey is good enough!) We used to joke among ourselves that Brent should run for office in Turkey. In short, you simply have to have been in Turkey and experienced this reaction to the Melungeons and their story to understand the fervor. So, although Brent and his Melungeon "band" are hardly household names even in prime "Melungeon territory" in America, never underestimate the resonance of the story with many Turkish people.

The evidence for the connection? Brent lays it out in his background chapter and in copies of several of his formal addresses in Turkey transcribed in a separate section of this book. The new DNA studies add a bit to the evidence for the connection, though it is not totally conclusive. I don't think I can say much about the link. It strikes me that there is a distinctive Mediterranean-Melungeon link, but it is less specifically Ottoman/Turkish in nature. This is not to say that I doubt that there is an Ottoman/Turkish-Melungeon link. My major problem with it is that there is no distinctive Ottoman/Turkic gene. The peoples of the Mediterranean, the Eastern Mediterranean in particular, and specifically Anatolia (the heartland of Turkey) are and have been for many centuries so ethnically mixed that they cannot be neatly divided up and discussed in purely national terms. Because people have been moving around the Mediterranean since well before the time of recorded history, certain kinds of distinctions are exceedingly difficult to make and prove in a convincing manner. The political borders do not match at all with clearly defined ethnic groups. The borders also have changed a good deal from period to period. Nowadays the Ottoman and modern Turks are definitely not a distinctive ethnic/racial grouping. Just go to Istanbul, Ankara, or Izmir and look at the people in the streets. There's a huge range of physical types. They mostly look "southern European" to me—that's the best I can say. So there is not going to be any DNA evidence to definitively prove the link. To the extent that there is a link, it likely will be cultural in both a broad and narrow sense more than anything else. Is there evidence of that? Definitely yes, but it also is not conclusive yet. But I do find it at least suggestive to observe as an outsider just how compatible the Melungeons and Turks I know feel with each other. And I'll add that it is very nice to see. They tend to take to each other very quickly.

I rather doubt that definitive evidence will ever be found of the Ottoman/Turkish-Melungeon link. What will accumulate with further studies over the next decade or two are many more pieces of evidence of the link in areas such as in cooking, language, music, folk stories, rug and clothing patterns, and so on. All of it together will be inadequate to convince the hardcore skeptics, but cumulatively it will be difficult to ignore and easily dismiss. What will occur is that there will be at least two "stories" about the Melungeons and their links. One will be the old, standard view of them as "triracial isolates." Far fewer people will believe in that any more. And there also will be a newer story. The evidence for a number of parts of it will leave many questions unanswered, but taken as a whole it will point to something more or less resembling a variation of the Melungeon tale with its Turkish-Melungeon link as presented in this book. The history books used in the public schools will present a version of the Melungeon story discussed here but critics of it will remain, as with most matters regarding what we call "history." *Everything* will never be known. It cannot be. Too much has been lost to be fully retrieved. At least, this is what I think is most likely to occur. Ultimately, the evidence will suggest which overall picture and specific details seem to be closest to the true state of affairs. Nobody should fear this. We should welcome the truth.

10. *What is the significance of the Ottoman/Turkish-Melungeon connection?*

Another question with a very complex answer. To begin with, the significance will be what people make of the connection, and that is not predictable. But let me give one sort of answer. Through the connection, people in America and Turkey will learn more about other peoples and, ultimately, themselves. It may spur them to travel more. They will not only learn things (knowledge) but also discover much to enjoy. They will become more fully an active part of the world. In terms of what we know about the world in which we live, we are all pretty much ignorant. Some are just a bit more ignorant than others. So the Turkish-Melungeon connection is a tie between peoples and certainly some stimulus to learning and feeling "outside the box," so to speak.

I cannot resist making a couple of personal remarks here. My sister, Harriette Ruth, lives on Long Island. When she heard about my Turkish connections and trips to that country, she started to ask people in the stores where she shopped whether they or their relatives had ever visited Turkey. She was amazed to find out how many people responded that they or others they knew happened, almost by accident, to visit Turkey, had known absolutely nothing about it, and had loved their time there and would gladly return. So it should not be surprising that as Melungeons learn more about their backgrounds that they are likely to have more to do with Turkey and the Turks, as will relatives and friends of these people. My sister is now quite interested in a number of aspects of Turkey and the lives of its people.

Another comment. When I was visiting Turkey, it struck me that Turks showed their approval and affection for the Melungeons by calling them "brother" and "sister" rather than "friend." The importance of kinship, however distant, was very important to our Turkish hosts and acquaintances and they viewed the Melungeons as kin, not just friendly, curious strangers. I had not expected this, but the Melungeons seemed to take to it as pretty natural behavior as well as gratifying. But I would not make too much of this observation.

What also was evident was that neither the Turks nor the Melungeons seemed to want anything in particular from each other. There was hardly any agenda on either side except to become acquainted and enjoy each other. The story itself has a fascination for the Turks I met. No, they agree that the link has not been conclusively shown by the available evidence, but they all know that Turks (Turkic peoples) have been great travelers for many centuries, and that they might have made it to the New World hundreds of years ago is interesting but not particularly surprising. They also are enchanted with the thought that they might have had kin who had played a role, however slight, in the development of an international superpower. And now that increasing numbers of them are traveling abroad and coming to the United States to work and/or to reside, it is grand to know that they probably have distant relatives already there. No matter that the Melungeons are not a numerous, powerful group. They exist, the ties are believed to exist, and further relationships will follow. As for what will become in the future, as the

Turks often say, *Inshallah* ("Whatever is God's will"). That is enough. So it is a relationship in the making at a number of levels. Certainly it has the promise of enhanced social, cultural, and educational exchange. And there may be some economic and political links also in the future.

11. *You have just mentioned a political link. Please say more about this.*

Certainly. One point before we begin. Virtually everyone on both sides was clear that the Turkish-Melungeon relationship should not involve formal governmental action or as some would call it, governmental interference. Nobody wanted formal governmental sponsorship which could easily slip into any sort of governmental control. Most Turks simply desired their government's distant benign approval and noninterference and the Melungeons did not even think of their American government becoming involved in their affairs. So when we discuss the political element, we aren't talking about a relationship controlled or directed by national governments.

Most of the Turks are concerned that Americans seem to be almost totally ignorant about Turkey, but when the American news media on rare occasions does mention their country it is almost always in a negative way. This bothers them and they feel it is most unfair. They also are concerned that there are several ethnic-interest groups in the U.S. that regularly attempt to sway the American government, especially Congress, to act in a manner harmful to valid Turkish interests. So, generally speaking, I would say that anything that presented any portion of the American people and/or its government with a better-balanced picture of Turkey and its people would be welcomed by all Turks. The Melungeons could help in this way by "spreading the word" without being involved in formal politics or acting as an interest group. Nobody I talked to expected the Melungeons to act as a unified interest group for assisting the Turks. But expanding the relationship between the Turks and Melungeons would almost naturally assist Turkey in that more Americans would know more about that country and discuss and act more fairly towards it and its interests. That in itself would be broadly beneficial.

I should also emphasize that almost no one expected the Melungeons to become a formal interest group and play pressure group politics. They do not have the potential capacity for that except in limited parts of a couple of states. Moreover, the Melungeons have shown little inclination to become organized for any purpose other than expanding their knowledge about their background, history, culture, family lines, and so forth. Although a handful of individual Melungeons might wish to form an interest group and press for achieving goals through direct, organized political action, this is highly unlikely to take place and there is no realistic likelihood of it occurring. The Melungeons I know are quite clear and vocal about this. The Turks who have met the Melungeons in Turkey have good reason to know it too.

The Turks are interested in the lobbying efforts of Turkish-Americans in the U.S. but very few of them know much about this and have no adequate basis for evaluating the efforts that are being made. Very few Turks understand the American governmental and political systems and American political culture. It is quite unlike anything they have ever experienced or learned in school. But increased contact between Melungeons and Turks would be a fine source of this information for the Turks both abroad and in America. Most Americans do not realize how distinctive their country's governments and politics are. They just take it all for granted and are surprised to learn that things are often done differently abroad. Although probably not directly very useful to Turkish lobbying efforts in the U.S., the Melungeon link could be indirectly useful in some ways.

12. *Please say a bit more about Turkish lobbying activities in the U.S. and relate it to the Turkish-Melungeon link.*

This is an interesting subject, worthy of study by itself. I am not an expert about it but let me make a few observations. First, although the U.S. and the Ottoman Empire/Republic of Turkey have had formal relations almost from the time of the creation of the United States, the relations were never very close. The relationship at the governmental level became closer after the end of World War II and with the start of the Cold War with the Soviet Union. The executive branches of the two governments and especially their militaries have had an extensive relationship for the past fifty-odd years but the countries as a whole have not been close. They've not been enemies; they simply haven't had that much contact.

Most the "lobbying" of the American government was done by members of the executive branches of the two governments with each other. This is the traditional manner. A strong, largely independent

Congress that affected American foreign/military policy in a multitude of ways was a new situation for the Turkish government that they were unprepared for. They had had no experience in dealing with anything like it before. In general, their efforts to positively influence Congress have not been nearly as successful as have their relations with the American presidency. They have tended to hire professional lobbyists to present their views to Congress and leave it at that. They seem to have little feel for how the American government works. In addition, the Turkish government seems to have little sense of public relations in America or how to influence the American people. They appear to deplore the idea that "all politics are local" and that how Americans feel about issues in congressional districts greatly affect how their representatives behave in Washington, D.C. The idea that the Turkish government should have a keen interest in affecting American public opinion so that American government policy is affected in ways favorable to them must be completely alien to most government officials in Turkey.

Much the lobbying now is the work of Turkish-American citizens/residents acting largely on their own. They have several definite handicaps. First of all, there aren't that many Turkish-Americans and most have arrived only in the last ten to fifteen years. They number about 300,000 now. Second, they are scattered around the country, not concentrated in a few areas to maximize their potential influence. Third, they have little experience in political organizing and lobbying in the American manner. To be effective in the U.S. requires organizational and informational skills that they had little opportunity to develop and practice in Turkey. Americans tend to be large-scale creators/joiners of organizations to assist them in achieving goals, some of them political in nature. This sort of civic participation hardly exists in Turkey. So Turkish-Americans will have to learn how to operate effectively in quite a different environment from the one they came from. The more Americans they can get to know and communicate frankly with, the more effective they will become over time. Of course, their children, brought up in America, will find all of this much easier and more natural.

One thing Turkish-Americans will need to do is just to become active in the civic affairs of their communities with no direct political objects in mind. This is basic public relations. The Turks I have met in my country have been fine people but Americans will not care about their thoughts, feelings, or goals, until they have come to know them personally and have worked with them on achieving common goals. Then relationships will form naturally as will future common actions. This means that Turkish-American lobbying only at the national and state levels has certain natural limitations. Creating effective political interest groups is a long-term operation. These have begun and I don't want to criticize them, especially considering how things were even a decade ago. Like groups that tend to be fairly effective in America, the Turkish-Americans must learn how to be part of the country's civic culture. They are fully capable of doing it but it will take time and energy and show relatively few payoffs for quite a while.

Now what does this have to do with Melungeons? Of course many Melungeons already understand their governmental and political systems quite well. They have grown up with them and have a good idea of what works and what doesn't. Many would be delighted to chat with Turks/ Turkish-Americans. Many Melungeons have contacts they can put these people in touch with. Turkish-Americans need to start networking, American-style, and Melungeons can assist with this. And politics is not the only area of importance. Turkish-Americans can use additional business contacts and much else. In short, the Melungeon link could be an asset in a number of ways that would be mutually valuable. But it is no panacea and too much emphasis should not be put on it. It can only be one of a number of elements. There are no guarantees of success, moreover. Melungeons can help Turkish-Americans play the American civic/ political game that few succeed at unless they play it well. But every group has to start where it is and with the assets it has. The Turkish-Melungeon link will be no stronger than people make it. And if it is not mutually beneficial, it has no chance. But please, let's not think of the linkage primarily in political terms; that is not what it is basically about.

13. *Could you sum up what this book is about?*

There are so many aspects to the subjects covered here. My own strong inclination is just to say that I hope many of its readers have found some information that has interested them, ideas to think about in the future that can used to broaden and deepen in positive ways the quality of their lives, and finally just wish everyone well. But we live in a country today where, in some places, we tell people what they are supposed to learn and then, at the end, check to see what they learned. How do you do this when the subject is so complex with various realities and with differing meanings for its readers? My basic instinct has always been just to present as much of the material as well as we could in a reasonably accurate and interesting manner and let everyone come away from it with what he or she chooses. It has already been clearly stated that the subject is not compact and tidy. It is difficult to organize and present. Much of the evidence for many of the key points cannot be laid out in these pages, but where this can be found has been printed here for anyone who desires to read further to locate it. Furthermore, practically everything needs additional study and discussion. But if we wait until everything is known, that might be decades, if ever. The book has been completed and every reader can evaluate it by his or her standards.

More than anything else, let me close with two main points. First, the book describes a process whereby groups of humans seek to make sense of and deal with aspects of their lives. As it is, some of these people and aspects cross boundaries of time and space. Some aspects link people together from different times and lands in previously unexpected ways. Not only are some of the specifics important, but so are the processes of learning, communication, and interaction. The basic Melungeon story is unfolding right now as is all of life. Much of life is involved but few would ever have expected to discover some of the combinations that are being found and developed. And before the initial creators of these patterns of interaction pass forever from the scene, it has seemed a worthy undertaking to present this record almost at the inception of the Turkish-Melungeon connection. No, it is unlikely to take up much space in the history books of the future but it is a genuine part of the present, it matters, and it will have consequences. It is a part of a history that never made its way into our textbooks. It is a lively stream springing from bits and pieces of knowledge that eventually will become rivers of awareness and an ocean of understanding. It is likely to have consequential effects on people's lives and so we believe it is worthy of notice. In these pages is a record of the first decade of the relationship with some words of a number of persons instrumental in its development to date.

Above all else, it is about the lives of people and the meaning of these peoples' lives to themselves and others. Truly, no man is an island sufficient by himself nor is any group isolated and self-sufficient. The Melungeons are part of the texture of American history and they are finding and redeveloping their place in it. Similarly, many of the people of Turkey are redefining themselves and their place in their country and the world. Two groups then, many of whose members are seeking to redefine themselves and their place in their countries and the world, have found that they have a good deal in common, more, in fact, than just a formal kinship link. This is the foundation on which their relationship will begin.

To the extent members of each group come to know each other, they are finding they have much they can easily share. And they quickly realize that they are not as alone in the world as they had thought. In fact, people of mixed backgrounds may well be a majority, not a minority of the people in the world. This creates a richness of cultures and possibilities but also insecurities that people who belong to one and only one group are less likely to develop.

In a way, the Melungeons and Turks are both "border peoples" with a great deal in common and much to share and mutually enjoy. Whether or not there is a specific genetic link, they in a larger sense have much in common and can be called "kin." The contact between them has now been made, and the next story will be of the relationship's development or nondevelopment. History is not fixed. They will make of the relationship what they *choose*. What they do matters. I wish all of them well, individually and collectively.